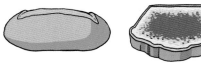

SANDWICHES!

CAPSTONE YOUNG READERS
a capstone imprint

TO MY DAD, WHO TAUGHT ME THE BEAUTY OF A GREAT
LUNCH SANDWICH, AND TO MY MOM, WHO STILL MAKES
ME SANDWICHES NOW. — AD

TO THE SAUCEMAN. SORRY THERE ISN'T MORE RANCH
DRESSING IN HERE. — BL

Sandwiches!: More Than You've Ever Wanted to Know About Making and Eating America's Favorite Food
is published by Capstone Young Readers
1710 Roe Crest Drive, North Mankato, Minnesota 56003
www.mycapstone.com

Library of Congress Cataloging-in-Publication Data

Names: Deering, Alison, author.
Title: Sandwiches! : more than you've ever wanted to know about making and
    eating America's favorite food / Alison Deering.
Description: North Mankato, Minnesota : Capstone Young Readers, [2017] |
    Audience: Age 9—13. | Audience: Grade 4—6. | Includes bibliographical
    references and index.
Identifiers: LCCN 2017008314 | ISBN 9781623708160 (pbk.)
Subjects: LCSH: Sandwiches—Juvenile literature. | LCGFT: Cookbooks.
Classification: LCC TX818 .D46 2017 | DDC 641.84—dc23
LC record available at https://lccn.loc.gov/2017008314

Designer: Bob Lentz
Editorial Director: Beth Brezenoff
Creative Director: Heather Kindseth
Production Specialist: Tori Abraham

Printed in China.
002075

SANDWICHES!

MORE THAN YOU'VE EVER WANTED TO KNOW ABOUT

MAKING

and
eating

AMERICA'S
FAVORITE FOOD

written by
ALISON DEERING

illustrated by
BOB LENTZ

TABLE OF CONTENTS

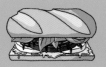

INTRODUCTION

(AKA WHAT IS A SANDWICH)

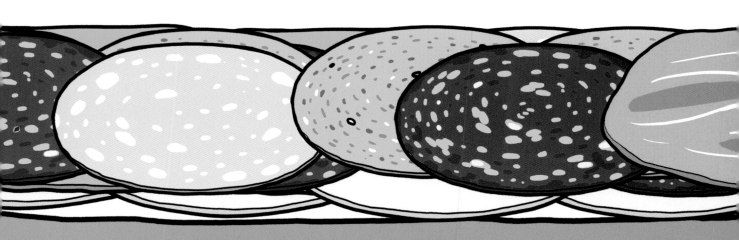

What is a sandwich? According to the United States Department of Agriculture, the "Product must contain at least 35 percent cooked meat and no more than 50 percent bread." The dictionary is slightly more open-minded, describing a sandwich as "two or more slices of bread or a split roll having a filling in between," meaning no meat required! (Good news for vegetarian sandwich-lovers everywhere!)

For our purposes, a sandwich is whatever you make of it! But no matter what, a great sandwich starts with the basics — the ingredients. Bookend your kitchen creation with the bread of your choosing — wheat, white, rye . . . you name it! But don't forget that what's between the bread is just as important — meat, cheese, and toppings can make or break a sandwich.

The beauty and genius of a delicious sandwich is that YOU as the chef and creator can make it anything you want it to be. And with this guidebook, you'll learn how to build the best sandwiches ever.

TOOLS

Making a sandwich is half the fun — obviously the main event is eating it!
It's also easy. All you need are a few key tools:

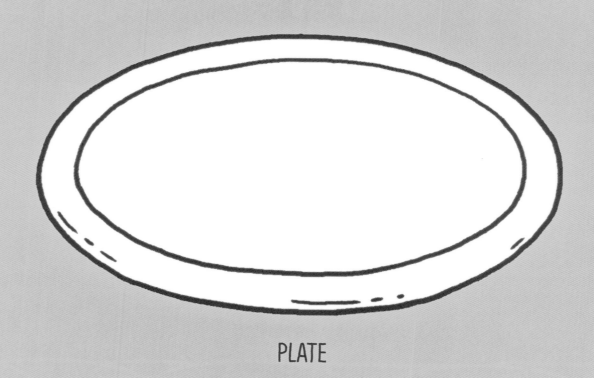

PLATE

BUTTER KNIFE

These will help you out too:

GRATER

MEASURING SPOONS

WOODEN SPOON

SPATULA

TONGS

CHEF'S KNIFE

BREAD KNIFE

SPOON

FORK

COLANDER

FRYING PAN

TOASTER

CUTTING BOARD

MIXING BOWL

SAUCE PAN

COOKIE SHEET

SLOW COOKER

PANINI PRESS

OVEN/BROILER

OVEN MITT

STOVETOP/RANGE

LEVEL 1

PLATE & KNIFE

Whether you're slicing bread, vegetables, or other ingredients, knife safety is a key component of cooking — and one of the first steps in becoming a sandwich-making superstar.

1. Start with adult supervision. If you've never used a sharp knife before, it's good to have a grownup around to help you.

2. Make sure you're at the right height. The countertop or cutting surface should be about waist-high. That way you can see what you're cutting. (Grab a stool if you need a boost!)

3. Get a good cutting surface. Using a clean cutting board is best for chopping, slicing, and dicing.

4. Make sure you're using a sharp knife. Dull knives are actually more dangerous because you have to apply more pressure in order to cut.

5. Hold your knife correctly. Use your dominant hand to grip the handle of the knife, keeping your fingers behind the bolster. (That's the thick part of the knife between the handle and the blade.) This is called a handle grip. Once you're more experienced, you can try the blade grip — gripping the knife with your thumb and index finger in front of the bolster.

6. Keep your other fingers out of the way. Make sure the hand holding whatever you're cutting is far enough back from the blade of the knife. Try folding the tips of your fingers under, so your knuckles are bent and facing out, on your non-moving hand.

CHEF'S KNIFE

This multipurpose knife comes in several different sizes and is good for a variety of kitchen-related jobs, including slicing and chopping vegetables, meat, and other ingredients.

BREAD KNIFE

A longer, thinner knife with a serrated blade. The teeth on the blade make slicing through bread without squishing or tearing easy. Serrated knives are also good for slicing tomatoes.

PB&J (PEANUT BUTTER & JELLY)

Peanut butter and jelly sandwiches — more commonly known as PB&Js — are a sandwich staple around the country. Chances are good that you've eaten at least a few in your lifetime. And while a PB&J might sound basic, it's anything but. The sweet jelly combined with the sticky, savory peanut butter make this classic sandwich practically irresistible.

GRAPE & STRAWBERRY are the most popular jams & jellies based on data from the U.S. Census Bureau.

60% of Americans surveyed prefer creamy peanut butter over crunchy.

APRIL 2

NATIONAL PEANUT BUTTER AND JELLY DAY

Peanut butter is a great source of protein — just 2 tablespoons contains 8 grams of protein!

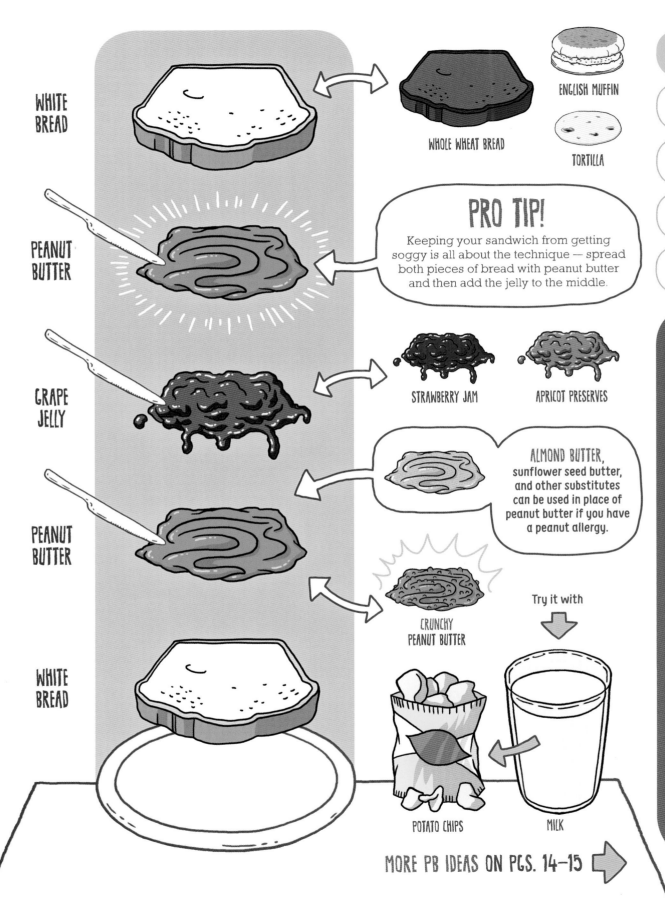

WHITE BREAD

WHOLE WHEAT BREAD

ENGLISH MUFFIN

TORTILLA

PEANUT BUTTER

PRO TIP!
Keeping your sandwich from getting soggy is all about the technique — spread both pieces of bread with peanut butter and then add the jelly to the middle.

GRAPE JELLY

STRAWBERRY JAM

APRICOT PRESERVES

ALMOND BUTTER, sunflower seed butter, and other substitutes can be used in place of peanut butter if you have a peanut allergy.

PEANUT BUTTER

CRUNCHY PEANUT BUTTER

Try it with

WHITE BREAD

POTATO CHIPS

MILK

MORE PB IDEAS ON PGS. 14–15 ➡

PB&J (PEANUT BUTTER & JELLY)

THE HISTORY OF THE PB&J

PB&J sandwiches may be a lunchbox staple in schools across the country, but that wasn't always the case. In fact, peanut butter used to be considered a delicacy. In the early 1900s it was served at upscale parties and fancy tearooms in New York. (Think peanut-butter-and-pimento and peanut-butter-with-watercress sandwiches.)

It wasn't until 1920 that the price of peanut butter dropped, and it became available to the masses, in part because sugar was added to the mix. Then, in the late 1920s, Gustav Papendick invented a process for slicing and wrapping bread, which meant kids (just like you!) could finally make their own sandwiches. Suddenly peanut butter sandwiches became a household staple.

Here's a brief breakdown of the life of a PB&J:

1884 — Marcellus Gilmore Edson, a Canadian, invents and patents peanut paste, made by milling roasted peanuts between two heated surfaces.

1893 — Peanut butter starts to gain popularity at the Chicago World's Fair.

1895 — Dr. John Harvey Kellogg patents a process for creating peanut butter from raw peanuts. He markets it as a healthy protein substitute for patients without teeth.

1901 — The first official reference to a peanut butter & jelly sandwich in the U.S. appears in *The Boston Cooking-School Magazine of Culinary Science and Domestic Economics*, thanks to Julia Davis Chandler.

1903 — Dr. Ambrose Straub of St. Louis, Missouri, patents a peanut-butter-making machine.

1920s — Sliced bread is invented! This invention takes sandwiches to the next level. Now kids can make sandwiches on their own.

1920s–1930s — Commercial peanut butter brands, including Peter Pan and Skippy, are introduced.

1930s — Peanut butter sandwiches become popular during the Great Depression, when many people needed a hearty, filling meal on the cheap. Peanut butter, which is packed with protein, became a more affordable substitute for meat.

1940s — Both peanut butter and jelly were part of U.S. soldiers' military rations; it's said that soldiers added jelly to their peanut butter sandwiches to make it more palatable. When those soldiers returned home, they helped the PB&J grow in popularity.

WE DARE YOU!

Peanut butter is great on its own, but a sandwich savant like you is probably ready to take it to the next level. Think you can handle the weird, the gross, the amazing, and everything in between? Here are just a few out-there options to experiment with . . . if you dare!

MAYO

CHEESE PUFFS

RAISINS

BUTTER

BOLOGNA

FRIED EGG

AMERICAN CHEESE

LETTUCE

PICKLES

POTATO CHIPS

15

BOLOGNA*

Whether you spell it "bologna" or "baloney," this sandwich has been a must-have in American lunchboxes for years, especially in the Midwest and South. Keep it simple, keep it basic. That's the beauty of bologna. Fussing it up with anything else is just . . . well, a bunch of baloney.

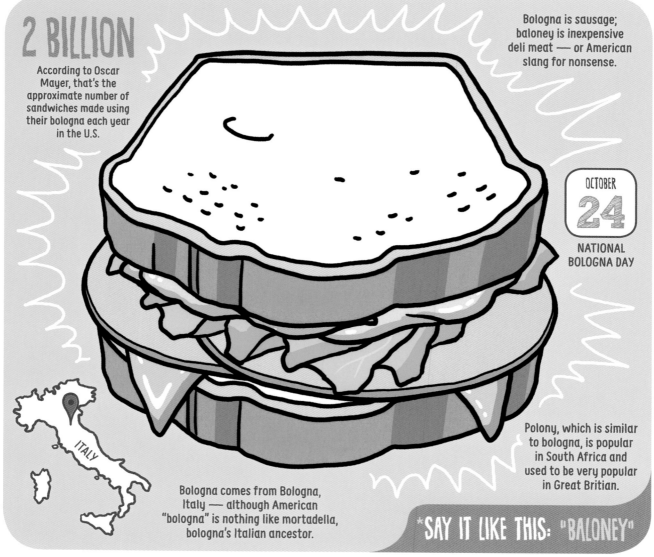

2 BILLION
According to Oscar Mayer, that's the approximate number of sandwiches made using their bologna each year in the U.S.

Bologna is sausage; baloney is inexpensive deli meat — or American slang for nonsense.

OCTOBER
24
NATIONAL BOLOGNA DAY

ITALY

Bologna comes from Bologna, Italy — although American "bologna" is nothing like mortadella, bologna's Italian ancestor.

Polony, which is similar to bologna, is popular in South Africa and used to be very popular in Great Britian.

*SAY IT LIKE THIS: "BALONEY"

WHITE BREAD

YELLOW MUSTARD

LETTUCE

BOLOGNA

AMERICAN CHEESE

WHITE BREAD

MAYO or KETCHUP — or both! — can also be used as condiments on a bologna sandwich.

I DARE YOU! Try adding PEANUT BUTTER to your bologna sandwich.

TRY FRIED BOLOGNA!

WHITE BREAD

PICKLES

AMERICAN CHEESE

THICK-CUT BOLOGNA

WHITE BREAD

Fry until brown and crispy!

SEE PG. 79 FOR SKILLET SAFETY!

BOLOGNA

CUCUMBER CREAM CHEESE

Cucumber cream cheese sandwiches are a staple of tea time, but the good news is, tea sandwiches aren't limited to just high tea. You can enjoy this light, tasty treat anytime you want! This version is made with thinly sliced crunchy cucumbers and smooth cream cheese. The best part is, you can have more than one!

2-3
The number of bites it should take to eat a tea sandwich.

Cucumber sandwiches originated in the United Kingdom.

FINGER FOOD
Tea sandwiches are meant to be a light snack before the main meal.

MORE TEA SANDWICHES!
- Smoked salmon & cucumber
- Prosciutto & asparagus
- Egg salad (see pg. 124)
- Tomato & cheddar

WHEAT BREAD

PRO TIP!
Cut the crusts off — or cut your sandwich into triangles, squares, or rectangles — to make your meal feel extra fancy!

 **WHITE BREAD** works just as well if that's what you prefer!

CREAM CHEESE

Use thin layers of cream cheese — it's just there to keep the bread from getting soggy.

RADISHES   DILL

CUCUMBERS

 Try using **ENGLISH CUCUMBER**. They don't have seeds, which means less water.

CREAM CHEESE

PIMENTO CHEESE

Pimento cheese, aka "the caviar of the South," is popular on sandwiches, crackers, veggies, and more in the southern U.S. Lucky for you, the basic recipe is easy to make at home!

2 cups shredded sharp Cheddar cheese
1/2 cup mayonnaise
1 (4-ounce) jar diced pimento, drained
salt and black pepper to taste

Mix all ingredients into a smooth or chunky paste and enjoy!

WHEAT BREAD

Try it with tea!

CUCUMBER CREAM CHEESE

TURKEY SWISS ROLLUP

If it doesn't exist between two slices of bread is it really a sandwich? That's a question for another time, but in this instance, we say yes! Rollup, wrap, sandwich-on-the-go — whatever you call it, this handheld turkey and Swiss treat is easy to make and even easier to eat. Use whatever type of tortilla or wrap you'd like (plain, whole wheat, sundried tomato, spinach, etc.), add the fillings, and wrap it up!

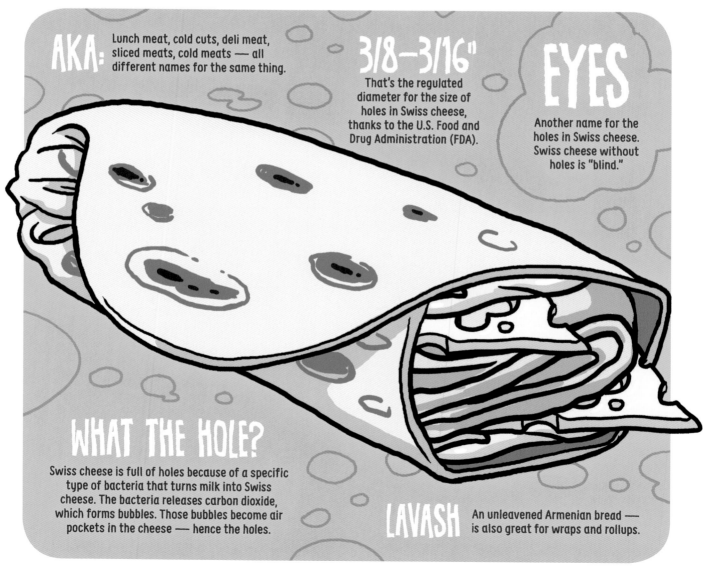

AKA: Lunch meat, cold cuts, deli meat, sliced meats, cold meats — all different names for the same thing.

3/8–3/16" That's the regulated diameter for the size of holes in Swiss cheese, thanks to the U.S. Food and Drug Administration (FDA).

EYES Another name for the holes in Swiss cheese. Swiss cheese without holes is "blind."

WHAT THE HOLE? Swiss cheese is full of holes because of a specific type of bacteria that turns milk into Swiss cheese. The bacteria releases carbon dioxide, which forms bubbles. Those bubbles become air pockets in the cheese — hence the holes.

LAVASH An unleavened Armenian bread — is also great for wraps and rollups.

TURKEY

SWISS CHEESE

MAYO

TORTILLA

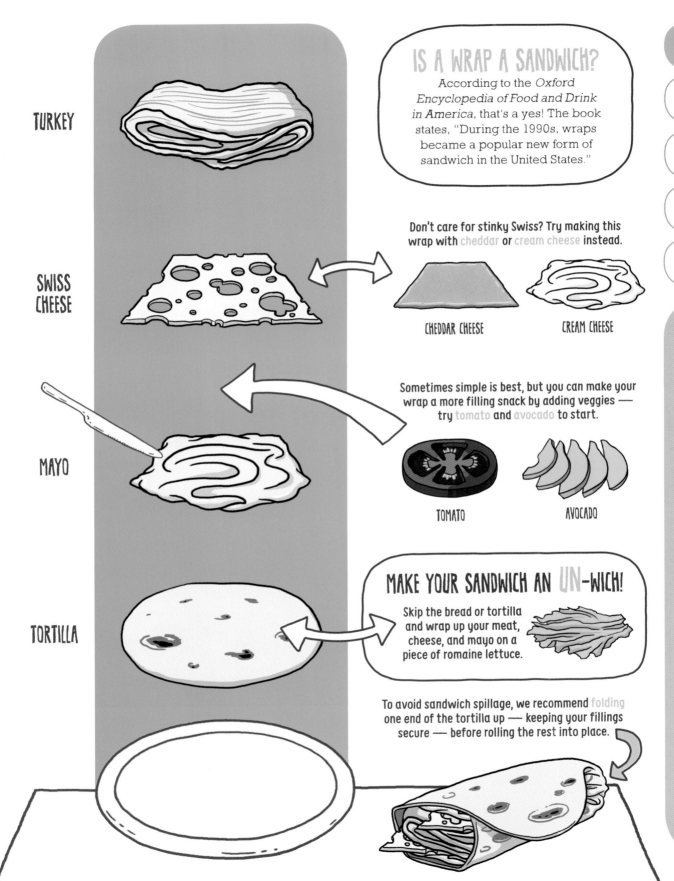

IS A WRAP A SANDWICH?

According to the *Oxford Encyclopedia of Food and Drink in America*, that's a yes! The book states, "During the 1990s, wraps became a popular new form of sandwich in the United States."

Don't care for stinky Swiss? Try making this wrap with cheddar or cream cheese instead.

CHEDDAR CHEESE

CREAM CHEESE

Sometimes simple is best, but you can make your wrap a more filling snack by adding veggies — try tomato and avocado to start.

TOMATO

AVOCADO

MAKE YOUR SANDWICH AN UN-WICH!

Skip the bread or tortilla and wrap up your meat, cheese, and mayo on a piece of romaine lettuce.

To avoid sandwich spillage, we recommend folding one end of the tortilla up — keeping your fillings secure — before rolling the rest into place.

TURKEY SWISS ROLLUP

HUMMUS

Hummus isn't just a dip for fresh veggies — with the amount of protein chickpeas pack, hummus has the strength to stand as the base for its own sandwich! Pile on crunchy veggies, like cucumber and sprouts, to contrast hummus's creamy texture. If you're feeling fancy, you can add falafel to your sandwich as well.

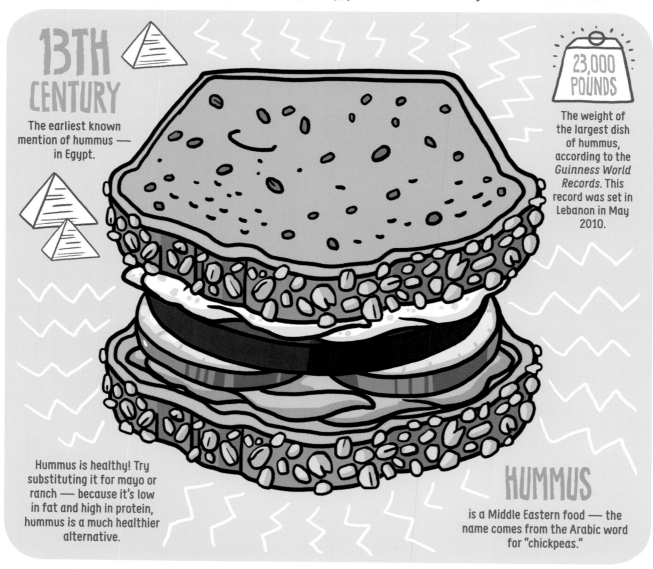

13TH CENTURY
The earliest known mention of hummus — in Egypt.

23,000 POUNDS
The weight of the largest dish of hummus, according to the *Guinness World Records*. This record was set in Lebanon in May 2010.

Hummus is healthy! Try substituting it for mayo or ranch — because it's low in fat and high in protein, hummus is a much healthier alternative.

HUMMUS
is a Middle Eastern food — the name comes from the Arabic word for "chickpeas."

MULTI-GRAIN BREAD

Try putting your hummus creation in a
PITA POCKET
rather than between bread.

TZATZIKI

Hummus and tzatziki can both be purchased in a grocery store or specialty market, but if you're feeling adventurous you can also try making your own!

TOMATOES

TZATZIKI RECIPE

Tzatziki (za-DZEE-kee) is a Greek sauce that's great on a sandwich or as a dip for fresh veggies — and it's easy to make at home!

1 1/2 cups Greek yogurt
2 garlic cloves, minced
1 cucumber, peeled and chopped
1/4 cup fresh mint leaves, chopped
2 Tbs. lemon juice
salt

Mix all ingredients together and let your dip sit for at least an hour.

CUCUMBERS

HUMMUS

HUMMUS RECIPE

1 can (15 ounces) chickpeas
1 garlic clove, minced
1/4 cup olive oil
2 Tbs. tahini
2 Tbs. lemon juice
salt, pepper, and paprika

Mix all ingredients together in a food processor, or use an immersion blender until smooth and creamy.

MULTI-GRAIN BREAD

PRO TIP!
Adding Greek yogurt to your hummus can make it creamier.

CHICKEN BROCCOLI ROLLUP

This chicken broccoli rollup uses a flour tortilla in place of bread. Just roll up your ingredients and you're ready to go! You can eat this "sandwich" cold, or pop it in the oven to heat things up. If you're eating it cold, we suggest adding hummus or cream cheese and leaving the broccoli raw. If you plan to bake it, stick with shredded cheddar and cook your broccoli before you add it to the wrap.

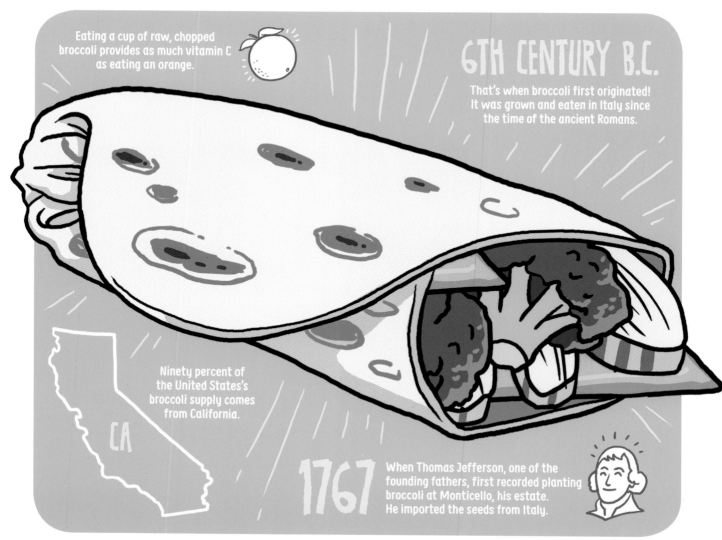

Eating a cup of raw, chopped broccoli provides as much vitamin C as eating an orange.

6TH CENTURY B.C.

That's when broccoli first originated! It was grown and eaten in Italy since the time of the ancient Romans.

Ninety percent of the United States's broccoli supply comes from California.

CA

1767 When Thomas Jefferson, one of the founding fathers, first recorded planting broccoli at Monticello, his estate. He imported the seeds from Italy.

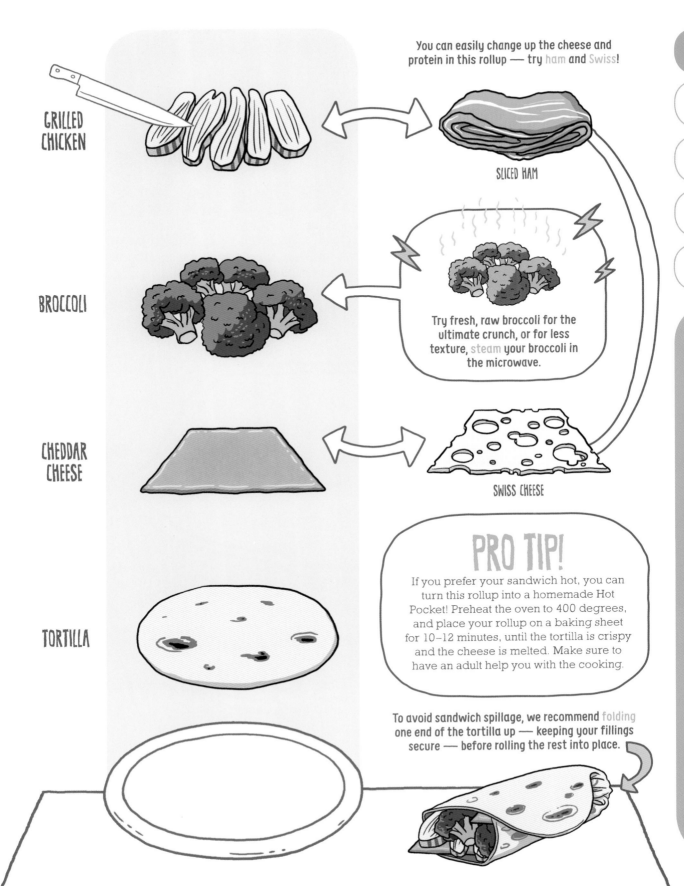

You can easily change up the cheese and protein in this rollup — try ham and Swiss!

GRILLED CHICKEN

SLICED HAM

BROCCOLI

Try fresh, raw broccoli for the ultimate crunch, or for less texture, steam your broccoli in the microwave.

CHEDDAR CHEESE

SWISS CHEESE

PRO TIP!

If you prefer your sandwich hot, you can turn this rollup into a homemade Hot Pocket! Preheat the oven to 400 degrees, and place your rollup on a baking sheet for 10–12 minutes, until the tortilla is crispy and the cheese is melted. Make sure to have an adult help you with the cooking.

TORTILLA

To avoid sandwich spillage, we recommend folding one end of the tortilla up — keeping your fillings secure — before rolling the rest into place.

CHICKEN BROCCOLI ROLLUP

HAM AND CHEESE

A ham and cheese sandwich is a classic, and the best part is, it's completely customizable! This version is made with cheddar, but any cheese will do — mozzarella, Swiss, American, you name it! You can also add as many toppings as you'd like. Start with lettuce, tomato, and onion, then add mayo, mustard, or both! If you're feeling fancy, try grilling your sandwich on the stove. It's an easy way to take a basic grilled cheese to the next level.

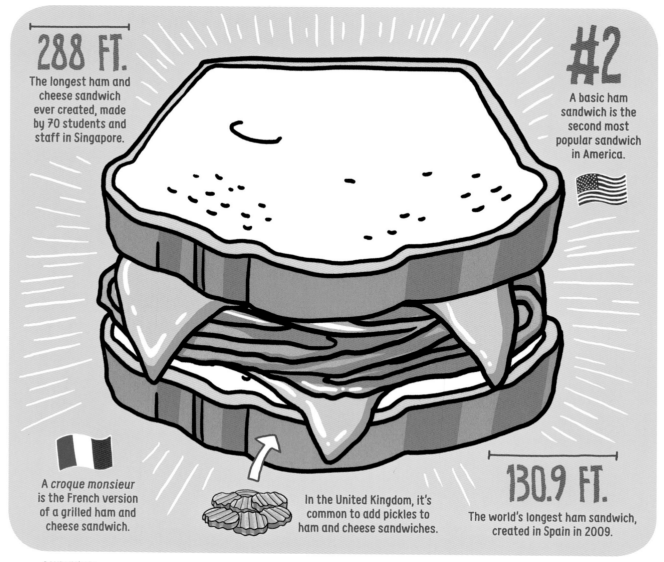

288 FT.
The longest ham and cheese sandwich ever created, made by 70 students and staff in Singapore.

#2
A basic ham sandwich is the second most popular sandwich in America.

A croque monsieur is the French version of a grilled ham and cheese sandwich.

In the United Kingdom, it's common to add pickles to ham and cheese sandwiches.

130.9 FT.
The world's longest ham sandwich, created in Spain in 2009.

WHITE BREAD

AMERICAN CHEESE

HAM

AMERICAN CHEESE

WHITE BREAD

Any type of bread will do — wheat, sourdough, etc. Keep in mind that a flatter bread is best for grilling purposes.

MUSTARD SCALE

Mustard, from mild to spicy, is a frequently used condiment in the quest for the perfect ham sandwich. Try these options on this or any sandwich:

HONEY

YELLOW

DIJON

SPICY BROWN

COARSE GROUND

JALAPEÑO

CHINESE HOT

FEELING CREATIVE?

Try adding thinly sliced apple or pear to your hot ham and cheese.

For apple, we suggest sticking with cheddar cheese.

Feel free to switch it up with mozzarella or Swiss cheese if you're using pears.

Try it with

TOMATO SOUP

SIDE SALAD

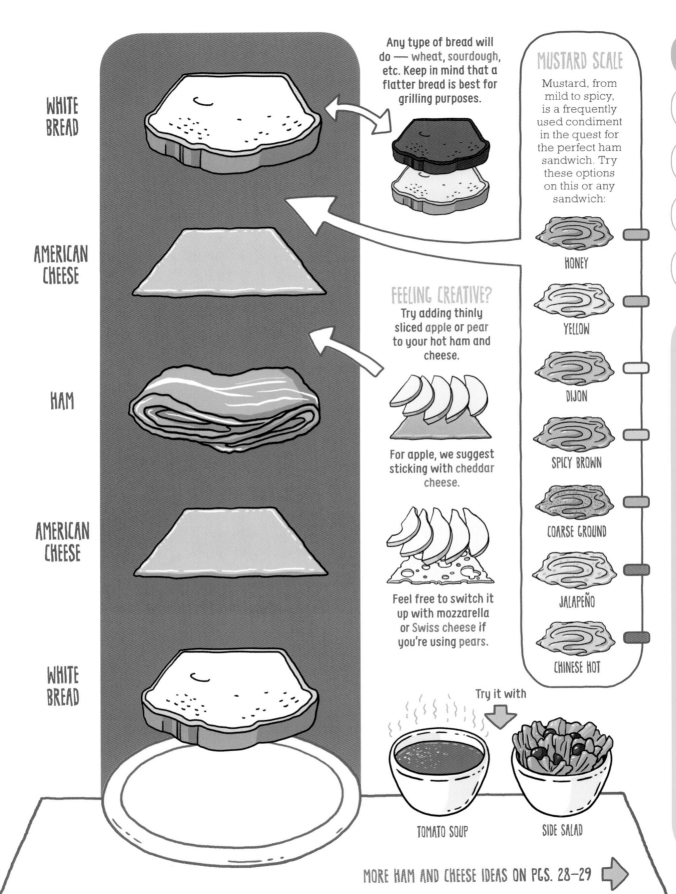

MORE HAM AND CHEESE IDEAS ON PGS. 28–29 ➡

HAM AND CHEESE

THE HISTORY OF THE HAM AND CHEESE

Sandwiches may be traceable all the way back to ancient times, but what type of sandwich claims the title of coming first? We may not know the specifics, but what we DO know is that the ham sandwich is one of the earliest known closed-face sandwiches. By 1850 London street vendors were selling it, and by 1894 the ham and cheese sandwich had made the jump to America. The sandwich was even sold at baseball games — along with ice cream and lemonade — in the 17th century. (It would take another fifteen years before hot dogs were introduced.)

But who's really responsible? According to the *Larousse Gastronomique 1961*, that would be Patrick Connolly, an eighteenth-century Irish immigrant to England. Connolly paired ham, Leicester cheese, and some type of mayo on a roll and started selling it. In some areas this might still be called "a Connolly."

Not one to let the Brits get a jump on them, the French likely started pairing ham and cheese on bread around the same time period. But it wasn't until the 20th century that they gifted us with their toasty version, the croque monsieur.

The ham and cheese has a lot to offer beyond being a basic, classic sandwich. You can also serve your ham and cheese hot — in fact, we recommend it! Just fire up your stove, butter the outsides of the bread, and grill it up until the outsides are crispy and the insides are melty. If you have a panini press you can also make your hot ham and cheese that way.

WE DARE YOU!

Ham and cheese is great on its own, but a sandwich savant like you is probably ready to take it to the next level. Think you can handle the weird, the gross, the amazing, and everything in between? Here are just a few out-there options to experiment with . . . if you dare!

CHOCOLATE

ICE CREAM

HONEY

CHEESE PUFFS

JELLY

PEANUT BUTTER

POTATO CHIPS

BANANAS

APPLE PIE FILLING

SAUERKRAUT

CAPRESE

Pizza, pasta, caprese — all the greats originate in Italy. The same goes for this delicious sandwich, a between-the-bread version of *insalata Caprese*, which literally translates to "salad of Capri" — a nod to the Italian isle on which it originated. A classic caprese sandwich is all about the ingredients: juicy tomatoes, fragrant basil, and fresh mozzarella. Typically served on a crusty baguette, this tasty treat is a vegetarian delight.

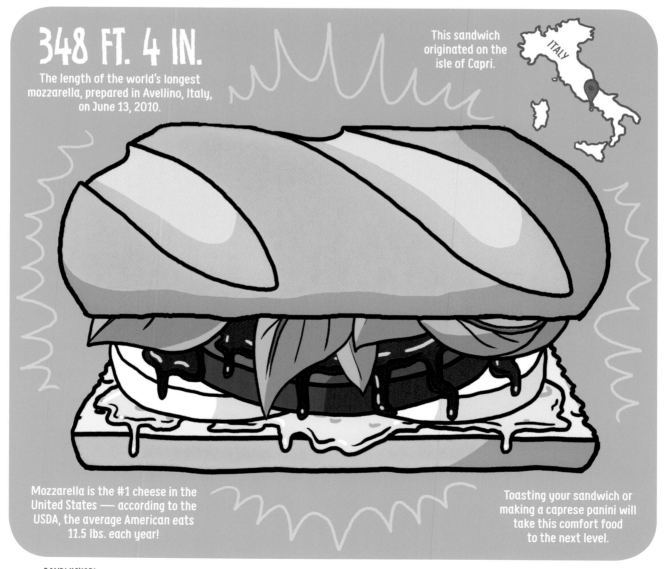

348 FT. 4 IN.
The length of the world's longest mozzarella, prepared in Avellino, Italy, on June 13, 2010.

This sandwich originated on the isle of Capri.

ITALY

Mozzarella is the #1 cheese in the United States — according to the USDA, the average American eats 11.5 lbs. each year!

Toasting your sandwich or making a caprese panini will take this comfort food to the next level.

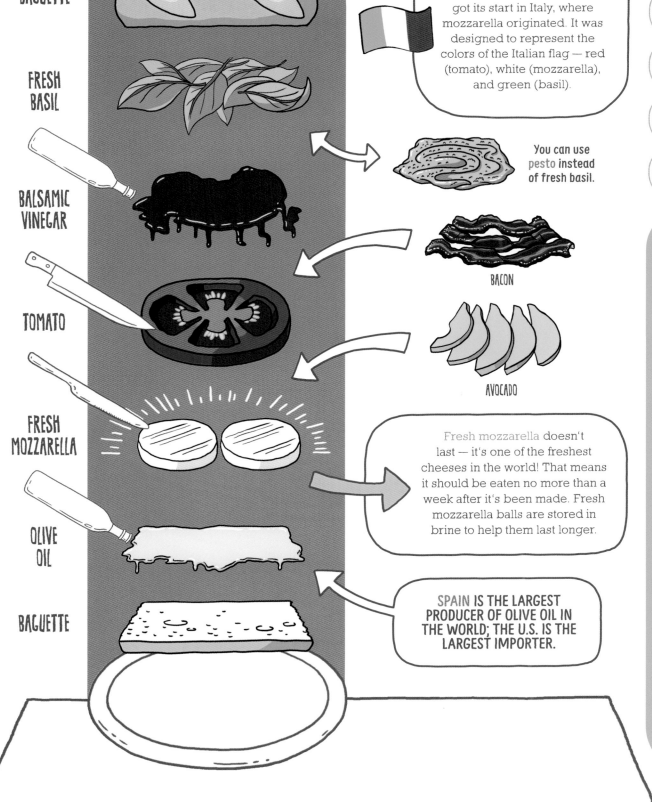

BAGUETTE

FRESH BASIL

1
2
3
4
5

DID YOU KNOW?
The caprese sandwich got its start in Italy, where mozzarella originated. It was designed to represent the colors of the Italian flag — red (tomato), white (mozzarella), and green (basil).

BALSAMIC VINEGAR

You can use **pesto instead of fresh basil.**

BACON

TOMATO

AVOCADO

FRESH MOZZARELLA

Fresh mozzarella doesn't last — it's one of the freshest cheeses in the world! That means it should be eaten no more than a week after it's been made. Fresh mozzarella balls are stored in brine to help them last longer.

OLIVE OIL

BAGUETTE

SPAIN IS THE LARGEST PRODUCER OF OLIVE OIL IN THE WORLD; THE U.S. IS THE LARGEST IMPORTER.

CAPRESE

31

FLUFFERNUTTER

The unofficial sandwich of Massachusetts, the fluffernutter is perfect for sandwich-lovers with a serious sweet tooth. Made from sweet marshmallow fluff (hence the "fluff") and creamy peanut butter (hence the "nutter") this sandwich is delicious when eaten for dessert, or even lunch if you're looking to switch it up from your standard PB&J.

1917

MA

Marshmallow Creme is invented by Archibald Query in Somerville, Massachusetts. He originally sold it door-to-door.

OCTOBER 8

NATIONAL FLUFFERNUTTER DAY falls on October 8th. Somerville, Massacusetts, still celebrates an annual Fluff Festival.

1913

Amory and Emma Curtis of Melrose, Massachusetts, invent Snowflake Marshmallow Creme.

The term "fluffernutter" can also be used to describe other sweet treats made with marshmallow fluff and peanut butter.

1960

The Durkee-Mower advertising agency coins the term "fluffernutter" so they have an easier way to market the sandwich.

WHITE BREAD

White bread is traditional for this soft, sweet sandwich, but you can also use wheat.

You can also get strawberry flavored fluff in some regions of the U.S.

MARSHMALLOW FLUFF

What is marshmallow fluff? Melted marshmallows and corn syrup blended together to create a spreadable treat.

I DARE YOU!

Try adding bacon to your fluffernutter. (If you're feeling less daring, try adding sliced bananas.)

PEANUT BUTTER

ALMOND BUTTER

NUTELLA

Peanut allergy? No problem! Just substitute another nut butter (like almond butter) in its place. You can also try this sandwich with Nutella.

WHITE BREAD

Wash it down with a cold glass of milk.

FLUFFERNUTTER

33

ICE CREAM

I scream, you scream, we all scream for ice cream! — ice cream sandwiches, that is. No meal would be complete without dessert, and no sandwich cookbook would be complete without an ice cream sandwich. You can customize this frozen delight any way you like. You pick the cookies, you pick the ice cream, you pick how many you can eat before brain freeze sets in.

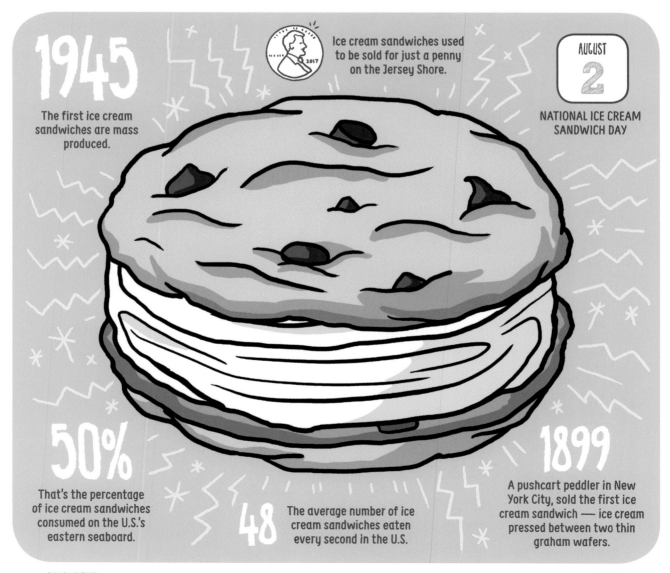

1945

The first ice cream sandwiches are mass produced.

Ice cream sandwiches used to be sold for just a penny on the Jersey Shore.

AUGUST 2

NATIONAL ICE CREAM SANDWICH DAY

50%

That's the percentage of ice cream sandwiches consumed on the U.S.'s eastern seaboard.

48

The average number of ice cream sandwiches eaten every second in the U.S.

1899

A pushcart peddler in New York City, sold the first ice cream sandwich — ice cream pressed between two thin graham wafers.

CHOCOLATE
CHIP
COOKIE

ICE CREAM

CHOCOLATE
CHIP
COOKIE

DID YOU KNOW?

This ice cream sandwich is technically called a Chipwich — ice cream sandwiched between two chocolate chip cookies — and was invented in 1981 by Richard LaMotta in New York City.

Make sure your ice cream is soft enough to scoop and spread, but not so soft it melts.

YOU PICK THE FLAVOR —
any type of ice cream will do!

VANILLA   CHOCOLATE

STRAWBERRY   MINT CHIP

Refreeze your sandwich as a whole once it's assembled.

Once you have your ice cream sandwich assembled, try rolling the edges in chocolate chips or sprinkles — they'll stick to the ice cream.

ICE CREAM

PESTO CHICKEN

Whether you're putting it on pizza, using it as a dipping sauce, or spreading it on a sandwich, pesto is one perfect creation. It also gives leftover chicken new life when slathered on Italian bread and paired with creamy mozzarella. Try making your own pesto, especially in the summer, when fresh basil is easy to find, making this scrumptious spreadable even more approachable.

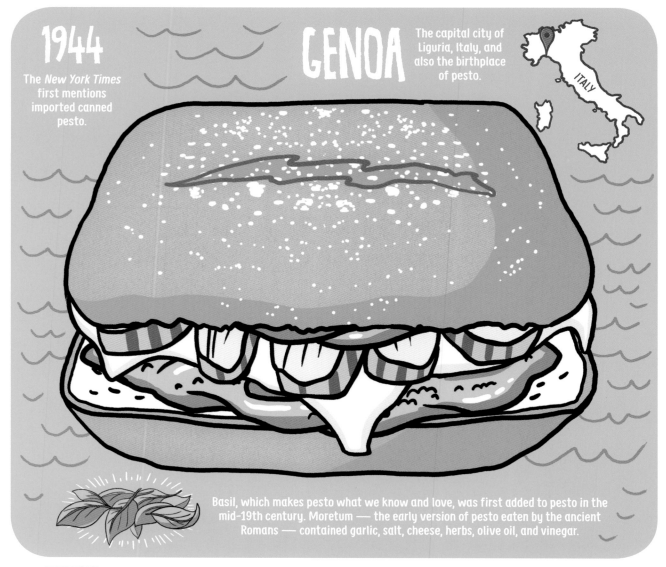

1944

The *New York Times* first mentions imported canned pesto.

GENOA

The capital city of Liguria, Italy, and also the birthplace of pesto.

ITALY

Basil, which makes pesto what we know and love, was first added to pesto in the mid-19th century. Moretum — the early version of pesto eaten by the ancient Romans — contained garlic, salt, cheese, herbs, olive oil, and vinegar.

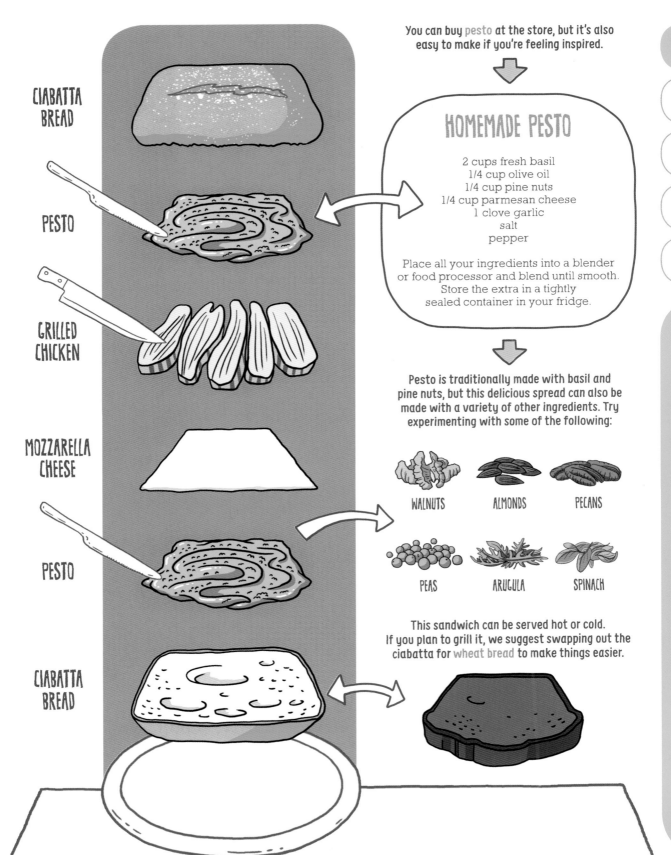

CIABATTA BREAD

PESTO

GRILLED CHICKEN

MOZZARELLA CHEESE

PESTO

CIABATTA BREAD

You can buy pesto at the store, but it's also easy to make if you're feeling inspired.

HOMEMADE PESTO

2 cups fresh basil
1/4 cup olive oil
1/4 cup pine nuts
1/4 cup parmesan cheese
1 clove garlic
salt
pepper

Place all your ingredients into a blender or food processor and blend until smooth. Store the extra in a tightly sealed container in your fridge.

Pesto is traditionally made with basil and pine nuts, but this delicious spread can also be made with a variety of other ingredients. Try experimenting with some of the following:

WALNUTS   ALMONDS   PECANS

PEAS   ARUGULA   SPINACH

This sandwich can be served hot or cold. If you plan to grill it, we suggest swapping out the ciabatta for wheat bread to make things easier.

PESTO CHICKEN

ROAST BEEF

A classic, comforting treat, the roast beef sandwich has been a Boston-area specialty since the 1950s. But it's been in existence long before that. Roast beef goes all the way back to jolly old England, where it's been eaten for at least two centuries. (It's the nation's signature dish.) And who can blame them? An easy-to-customize roast beef sandwich, like this beef and cheddar version, is something you want to take credit for.

1877

A recipe for "Beefsteak Toast" — an early version of the roast beef sandwich — is published.

What's in a name? Arby's actually stands for R.B., the initials of the Raffel brothers — and coincidentally, roast beef.

1951

Kelly's Roast Beef, a Boston-area restaurant, claims to have invented the roast beef sandwich this year.

Roast beef sandwiches can be eaten hot or cold!

1964

Arby's was founded, taking the roast beef sandwich mainstream — or at least making it fast food.

Why roast beef? The Raffel brothers, the founders of Arby's, were inspired by a $0.79 roast beef sandwich, which they found at a Boston-area sandwich shop one rainy Halloween night.

HAMBURGER BUN

CHEDDAR CHEESE

ROAST BEEF

HAMBURGER BUN

Serve with a side of leftover mashed potatoes or french fries.

OTHER ROAST BEEF VARIATIONS:

CORNED BEEF

PASTRAMI

FRENCH DIP
(See pg. 130)

HORSERADISH SAUCE

GRILLED ONIONS

TOMATO

LETTUCE

PROVOLONE CHEESE

SWISS CHEESE

BEEF ON WECK

Typically found in western New York, the beef on weck is a regional take on the traditional roast beef sandwich. This version is made with rare, thinly sliced roast beef and horseradish piled on a kummelweck roll — a kaiser roll topped with pretzel salt and caraway seeds.

Open up the sandwich and drop the leftover mashed and gravy on top to make a hot beef commercial!

ROAST BEEF

FRIED CHICKEN

Fried chicken is the ultimate comfort food, and now you can even enjoy it in sandwich form! You don't have to fire up the deep fryer either — this easy-to-make (and even easier-to-enjoy) sandwich is made using leftover chicken fingers, which are just as delicious cold. (If you prefer yours hot — or you're fresh out of leftovers — you can easily heat some up in the oven. Check out the safety tips on pgs. 68–69 first.)

JULY 6

NATIONAL FRIED CHICKEN DAY

1952

"Colonel" Harland Sanders opens the first Kentucky Fried Chicken restaurant.

Up until the early 1900s, fried chicken was reserved for special occasions.

People used to believe chickens could see the future. After all, they're the only animals that announce daybreak.

There are more chickens on Earth than there are people.

Scottish immigrants first brought fried chicken to the United States — most other cultures baked chicken.

The earliest recipe for what Americans know as fried chicken was actually published in a British cookbook, *The Art of Cookery Made Plain and Easy.*

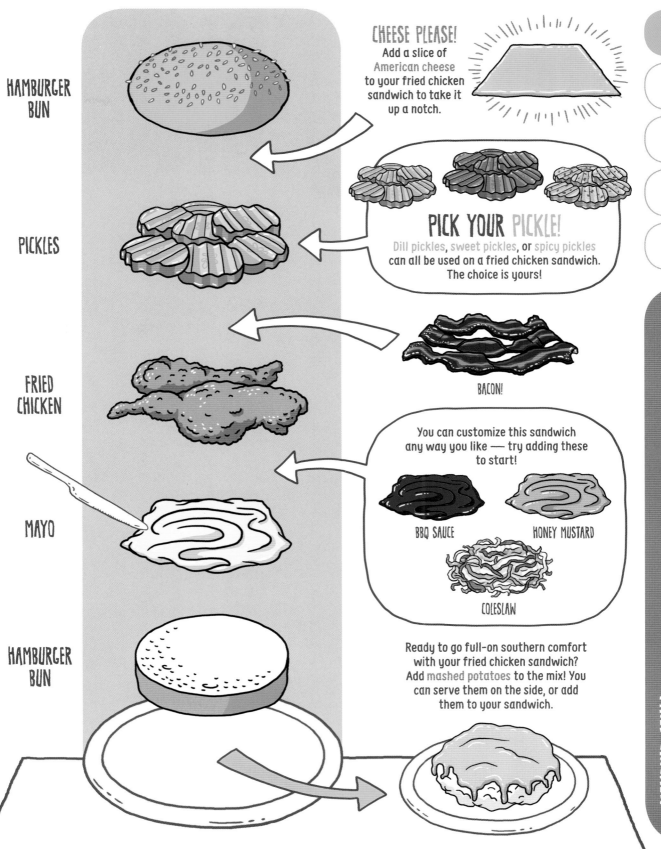

HAMBURGER
BUN

PICKLES

FRIED
CHICKEN

MAYO

HAMBURGER
BUN

CHEESE PLEASE!
Add a slice of American cheese to your fried chicken sandwich to take it up a notch.

PICK YOUR PICKLE!
Dill pickles, sweet pickles, or spicy pickles can all be used on a fried chicken sandwich. The choice is yours!

BACON!

You can customize this sandwich any way you like — try adding these to start!

BBQ SAUCE   HONEY MUSTARD

COLESLAW

Ready to go full-on southern comfort with your fried chicken sandwich? Add mashed potatoes to the mix! You can serve them on the side, or add them to your sandwich.

BUFFALO CHICKEN

Ready to spice things up? A kick of hot, spicy buffalo sauce takes this chicken sandwich up a notch. While buffalo sauce is most commonly associated with buffalo wings, the flavor is just as good when eaten between bread. Lettuce, sour cream, and blue cheese can all help balance the heat a little bit, but how spicy your sandwich turns out is up to you.

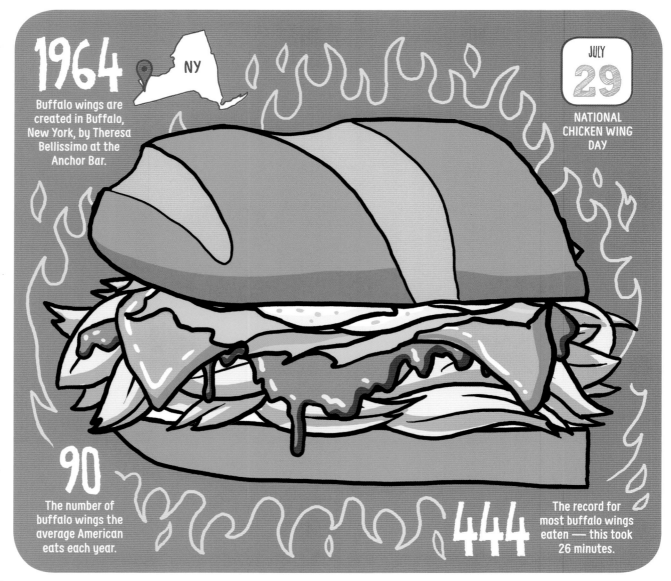

1964 NY

Buffalo wings are created in Buffalo, New York, by Theresa Bellissimo at the Anchor Bar.

JULY 29

NATIONAL CHICKEN WING DAY

90

The number of buffalo wings the average American eats each year.

444

The record for most buffalo wings eaten — this took 26 minutes.

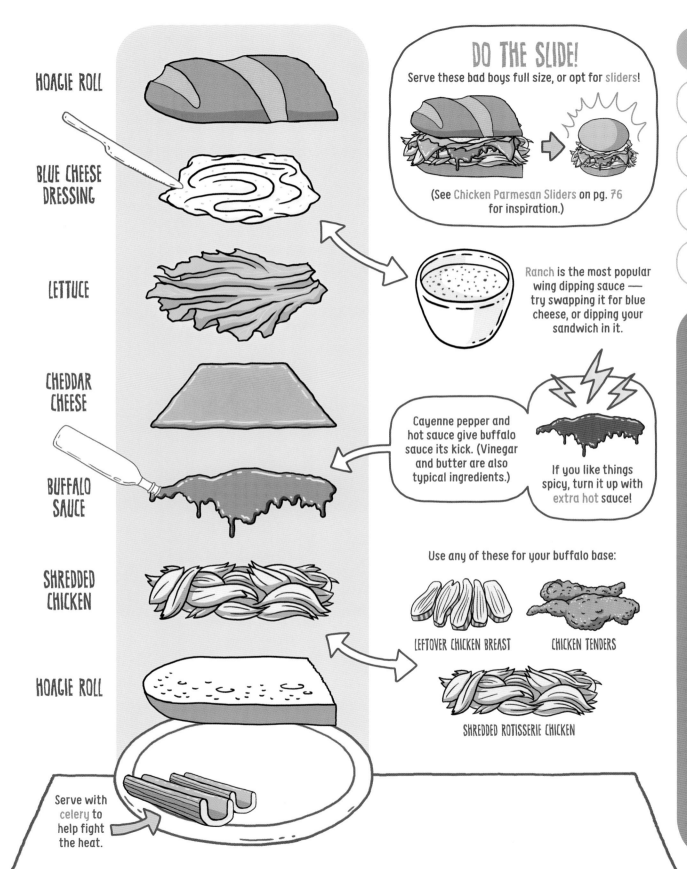

HOAGIE ROLL

BLUE CHEESE DRESSING

LETTUCE

CHEDDAR CHEESE

BUFFALO SAUCE

SHREDDED CHICKEN

HOAGIE ROLL

DO THE SLIDE!

Serve these bad boys full size, or opt for sliders!

(See Chicken Parmesan Sliders on pg. 76 for inspiration.)

Ranch is the most popular wing dipping sauce — try swapping it for blue cheese, or dipping your sandwich in it.

Cayenne pepper and hot sauce give buffalo sauce its kick. (Vinegar and butter are also typical ingredients.)

If you like things spicy, turn it up with extra hot sauce!

Use any of these for your buffalo base:

LEFTOVER CHICKEN BREAST

CHICKEN TENDERS

SHREDDED ROTISSERIE CHICKEN

Serve with celery to help fight the heat.

BUFFALO CHICKEN

STUFFED FRENCH TOAST

French toast isn't strictly a breakfast food anymore. It's easy to take your leftover French toast and turn it into a delicious sandwich and brand-new meal. Similar to the Monte Cristo, minus the meat, this stuffed version combines sweet strawberries and cream cheese for a scrumptious stuffed sandwich. (If you want to make fresh French toast, check out the recipe on pg. 105.)

4TH CENTURY

The first recipe for French toast appears in *Apicius*, a cookbook with a collection of ancient Roman recipes.

The French name "pain perdu" means "lost bread" — this refers to the fact that French toast is a way to use up stale bread, which would otherwise be lost.

NOVEMBER
28
NATIONAL FRENCH TOAST DAY

FRENCH
TOAST

DID YOU KNOW?
French toast is also known as German toast, eggy bread, gyspy toast, french-fried bread, and more!

CREAM
CHEESE

Try substituting different fruits — these would also work well:

STRAWBERRIES

BANANAS   PEACHES

POWDERED
SUGAR

PEARS   APPLES

FRENCH
TOAST

PRO TIP!
If you're making your French toast fresh, day-old bread is best.

STRAWBERRIES

Don't have fresh strawberries? Try using preserves or jam instead.

CREAM
CHEESE

FRENCH
TOAST

Sprinkle more powdered sugar on top, and serve with a side of syrup for dipping.

STUFFED FRENCH TOAST

ROASTED VEGGIE

You don't have to fire up the grill or oven to enjoy a roasted veggie sandwich. Like many sandwiches, the beauty is in the simplicity — roasted vegetables from a jar or can will work just as well. And you pick what sounds good — roasted red peppers, zucchini, mushrooms, and more can be used to beef up this meatless meal. Spinach, arugula, or romaine lettuce adds some crunch, while tangy goat cheese rounds things out.

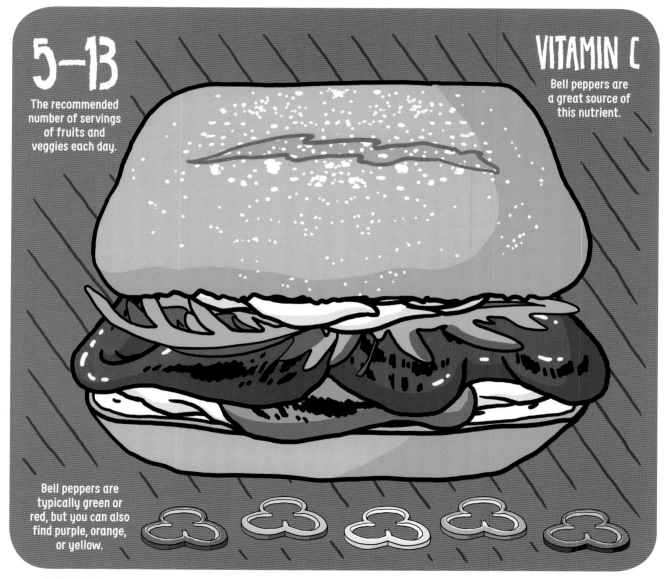

5-13
The recommended number of servings of fruits and veggies each day.

VITAMIN C
Bell peppers are a great source of this nutrient.

Bell peppers are typically green or red, but you can also find purple, orange, or yellow.

CIABATTA

GOAT CHEESE

ARUGULA

ROASTED RED PEPPERS

ROASTED GREEN PEPPERS

GOAT CHEESE

CIABATTA

Arugula has a peppery kick — if that's not for you, try using spinach, romaine lettuce, or another green that sounds yummy!

ZUCCHINI

MUSHROOMS

TOMATO

ONION

Not a vegetarian? Try adding bacon to your sandwich.

If you have a panini press handy, you can turn this sandwich into a warm snack!

ROASTED VEGGIE

TURKEY LEFTOVERS ("THE GOBBLER")

Stuffing your face with turkey is quite possibly the best part of Thanksgiving — or any holiday, for that matter. But second best? The leftovers, hands down! And now you have the perfect sandwich to incorporate all your holiday favorites — leftover turkey, gravy, stuffing, and cranberry sauce — into one mouthwatering meal. Now that's something to be thankful for.

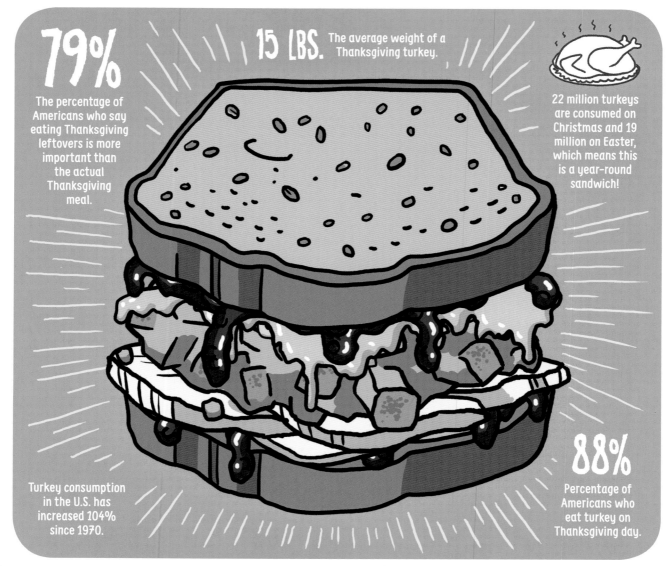

79%
The percentage of Americans who say eating Thanksgiving leftovers is more important than the actual Thanksgiving meal.

15 LBS. The average weight of a Thanksgiving turkey.

22 million turkeys are consumed on Christmas and 19 million on Easter, which means this is a year-round sandwich!

Turkey consumption in the U.S. has increased 104% since 1970.

88%
Percentage of Americans who eat turkey on Thanksgiving day.

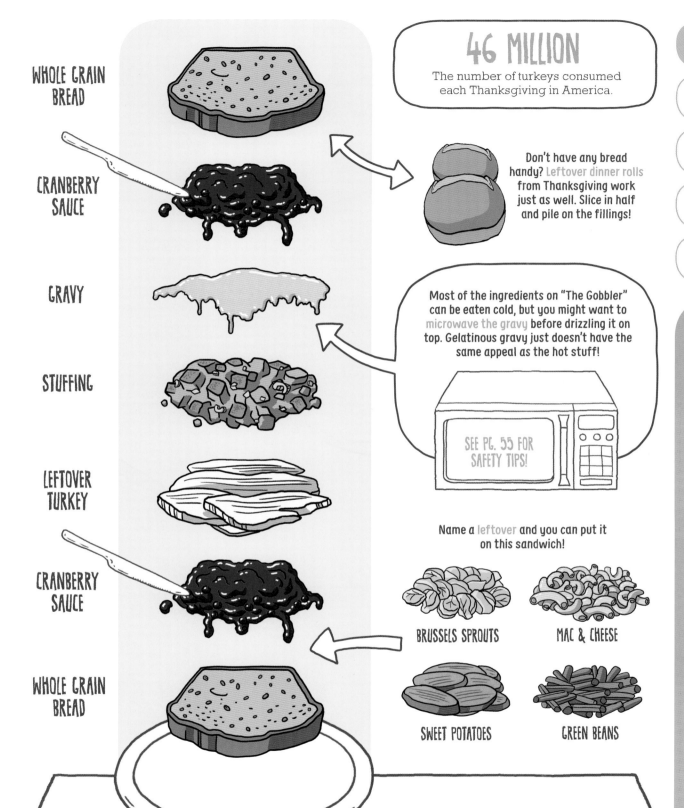

WHOLE GRAIN BREAD

CRANBERRY SAUCE

GRAVY

STUFFING

LEFTOVER TURKEY

CRANBERRY SAUCE

WHOLE GRAIN BREAD

46 MILLION

The number of turkeys consumed each Thanksgiving in America.

Don't have any bread handy? Leftover dinner rolls from Thanksgiving work just as well. Slice in half and pile on the fillings!

Most of the ingredients on "The Gobbler" can be eaten cold, but you might want to microwave the gravy before drizzling it on top. Gelatinous gravy just doesn't have the same appeal as the hot stuff!

SEE PG. 55 FOR SAFETY TIPS!

Name a leftover and you can put it on this sandwich!

BRUSSELS SPROUTS

MAC & CHEESE

SWEET POTATOES

GREEN BEANS

TURKEY LEFTOVERS ("THE GOBBLER")

MUFFULETTA*

Make way for the muffuletta! This regional sandwich got its start in the Big Easy, aka New Orleans, Louisiana, and remains a specialty there to this day. Interestingly enough, despite the muffuletta having a decidedly Italian background, the sandwich is nowhere to be found in Italy. So how do you eat it? A muffuletta is typically served at room temperature, and while some may protest, we say there's nothing wrong with toasting yours up if the mood strikes.

The sandwich was not always called a muffuletta — the name carried over from the muffuletto bread the sandwich was made on.

LATE 1800S–EARLY 1900S

The muffuletta is the brainchild of Sicilian immigrants, who arrived and settled in New Orleans.

LA

1906

The first muffuletta sandwich was made by Salvatore Lupo at Central Grocery, his specialty market in New Orleans's French Quarter.

10"

The approximate diameter of a loaf of muffuletta bread.

SAY IT LIKE THIS: "MOO-FU-LEHT-UH"

SICILIAN SESAME BREAD

OLIVE SALAD

PROVOLONE

HAM

MOZZARELLA

SALAMI

MORTADELLA

OLIVE SALAD

SICILIAN SESAME BREAD

Muffuletta loaf is a wide, round, flat bread covered in sesame seeds — sort of like a cross between focaccia and French bread. Semolina rolls work well if you have access to a good bakery.

OLIVE SALAD

You can buy olive salad at the store, but wouldn't you also like to know what you're eating?

Olive salad is made up of chopped green olives, black olives, celery, cauliflower, carrots, sweet peppers, onions, capers, parsley, pepperoncini, oregano, garlic, vinegar, herbs, and spices. (Similar to the giardiniera you'll find on an Italian beef.)

Spread this on the inside of both slices of bread in a thick layer.

You can also add olive salad to your pizza sandwich (see pg. 90) if you like the taste!

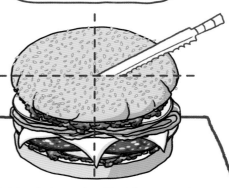

A full ten-inch round muffuletta is a hearty meal. Try cutting yours into quarters.

CLASSIC ITALIAN

A classic Italian sub sandwich is practically an art form, and what's even more beautiful is that this sandwich is just as good enjoyed at home as it is at an old-school Italian deli. Picture cold cuts piled high on a hoagie roll, topped with lettuce, tomato, and onion, and drizzled with oil and vinegar. The hardest part about enjoying this sandwich just might be fitting it in your mouth.

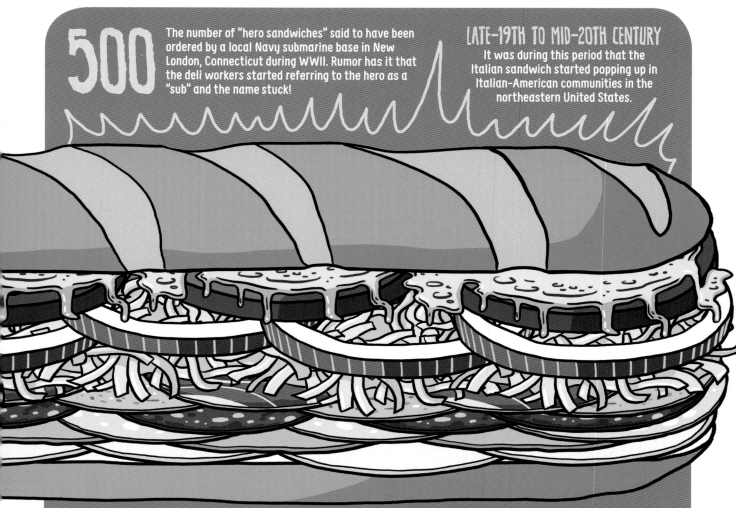

500
The number of "hero sandwiches" said to have been ordered by a local Navy submarine base in New London, Connecticut during WWII. Rumor has it that the deli workers started referring to the hero as a "sub" and the name stuck!

LATE-19TH TO MID-20TH CENTURY
It was during this period that the Italian sandwich started popping up in Italian-American communities in the northeastern United States.

ME
Portland, Maine, claims to be the birthplace of the Italian sandwich — it's the state's signature sammie.

1902 The year Giovanni Amato, a baker, invented the Italian sandwich in Portland, Maine.

1965
The first Subway sandwich shop opened.

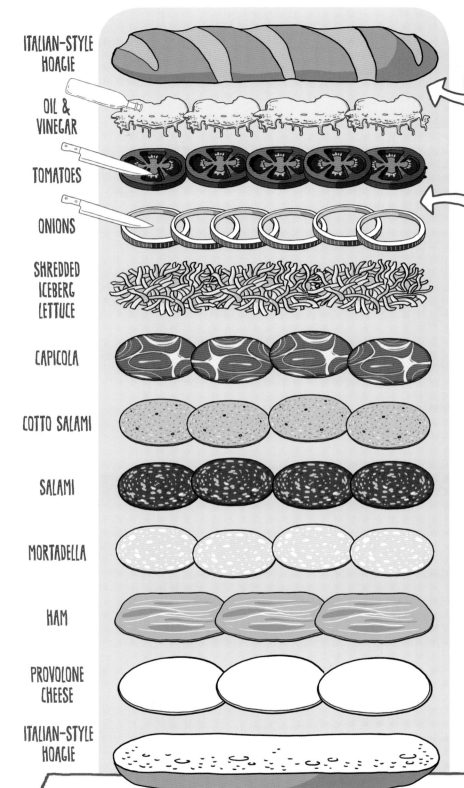

ITALIAN-STYLE HOAGIE

OIL & VINEGAR

TOMATOES

ONIONS

SHREDDED ICEBERG LETTUCE

CAPICOLA

COTTO SALAMI

SALAMI

MORTADELLA

HAM

PROVOLONE CHEESE

ITALIAN-STYLE HOAGIE

PRO TIP!

Bookend your Italian sub with an extra pieces of cheese on top to keep the bread from getting soggy.

You can also add hot peppers to your classic Italian sub if you like things a little spicy.

Or try sweet peppers for a milder taste.

WHAT'S IN A NAME?

The classic Italian has more than a dozen regional identifiers in the U.S. A submarine sandwich is most common, but which one do you use?

HOAGIE	Philadelphia
HERO	New York
GRINDER	New England
BLIMPIE	New Jersey
ZEPPELIN	Eastern Pennsylvania
TORPEDO	New York or New Jersey
WEDGE	Upstate New York
GATSBY	Cape Town, South Africa

Try it with

POTATO CHIPS

COLA

CLASSIC ITALIAN

LEVEL 2

TOASTER & MICROWAVE

Congratulations! You did it — you made it to Level 2! Now that you've mastered your basic plate-and-knife sandwiches, it's time to move on to a couple of kitchen appliances: the toaster and the microwave.

The toaster and the microwave can be found in nearly every kitchen, and you'd be surprised at what a difference they can make in your sandwich creating. These handy heating tools can take sandwiches from cold to hot and make leftovers edible again! Before you dive into Level 2's scrumptious sandwiches, check out a few microwave and toaster tips to keep you safe in the kitchen:

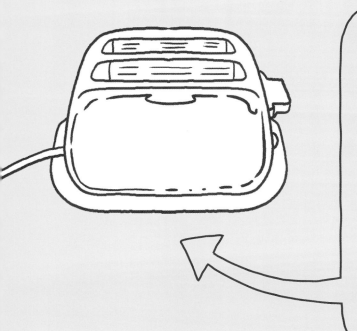

TOASTER SAFETY:

- Toasters get hot — make sure to keep it away from anything that could catch fire, like paper towels or kitchen towels.

- As a general rule, toasters are for making toast. Stick to using yours for bread and bagels, the outside sandwich components. (Nothing that melts — like cheese! — should go into the toaster.)

- If toast gets stuck, unplug the toaster. Never use metal utensils to remove food from the toaster. (If you have wooden toaster tongs, use those.)

- Toasters can catch on fire. If you see flames from any kitchen appliance, get help immediately.

- Wait for your toaster to cool before putting it away — the top and sides can get warm and you don't want to burn yourself.

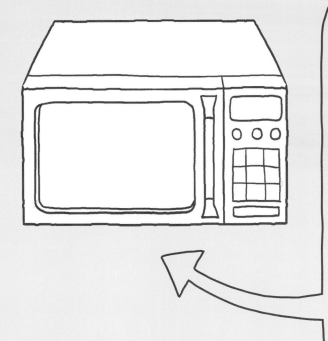

MICROWAVE SAFETY:

- Don't use a microwave while it's empty — that means no running it if there's no food in it.

- Never put metal, including foil, metallic wrappers, or silverware in the microwave.

- Use only microwave-safe cookware. (The FDA recommends using glass, ceramic, and plastic containers labeled for microwave oven use.)

- Make sure to read and follow directions carefully and know how to use the microwave controls. (Things like power level, quick start, etc. are important)

- Even if you've only microwaved something for a short amount of time, food coming out of the microwave can be hot. Let your food cool slightly before eating so you don't burn your mouth.

- Just like food gets hot in the microwave, so will the plate or container you used. It's a good idea to keep potholders handy to remove hot dishes.

BLT (BACON, LETTUCE, TOMATO)

Nothing says summer like a BLT. Farm-fresh tomatoes pair perfectly with crispy, greasy bacon and cool, refreshing lettuce. And the best part is, a BLT is a sandwich best enjoyed at home. Just toast your bread, pile on your ingredients, and pull up a seat — preferably at an outdoor table — to enjoy!

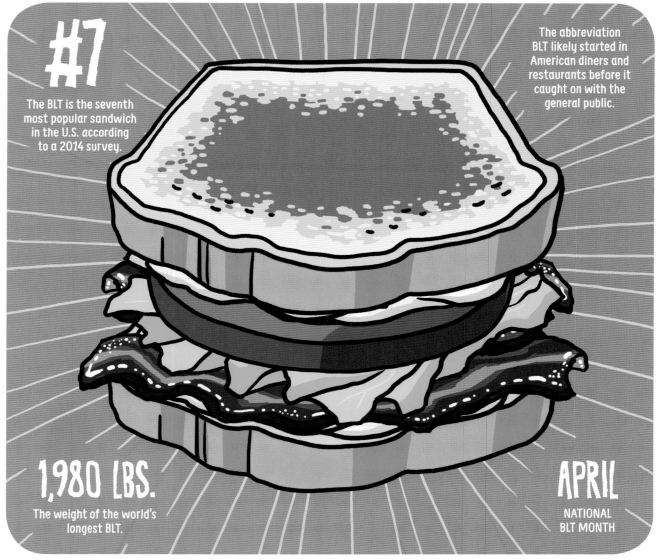

#7
The BLT is the seventh most popular sandwich in the U.S. according to a 2014 survey.

The abbreviation BLT likely started in American diners and restaurants before it caught on with the general public.

1,980 LBS.
The weight of the world's longest BLT.

APRIL
NATIONAL BLT MONTH

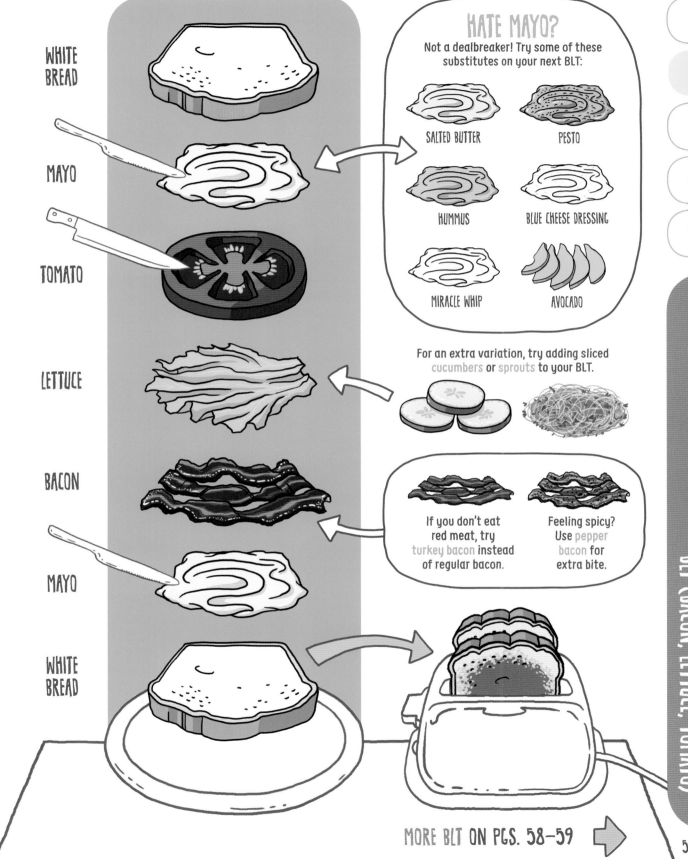

WHITE BREAD

MAYO

TOMATO

LETTUCE

BACON

MAYO

WHITE BREAD

HATE MAYO?

Not a dealbreaker! Try some of these substitutes on your next BLT:

SALTED BUTTER

PESTO

HUMMUS

BLUE CHEESE DRESSING

MIRACLE WHIP

AVOCADO

For an extra variation, try adding sliced cucumbers or sprouts to your BLT.

If you don't eat red meat, try turkey bacon instead of regular bacon.

Feeling spicy? Use pepper bacon for extra bite.

MORE BLT ON PGS. 58–59

BLT (BACON, LETTUCE, TOMATO)

BETWEEN THE BREAD:

THE HISTORY OF THE BLT

Given all the casual, delicious glory that goes along with BLTs, you might be surprised to learn that they did not actually start out as a casual sandwich. In fact, BLTs are actually a distant descendant of Victorian-era tea sandwiches. (And you can't get much fancier than a Victorian-era tearoom!) Many of the facts behind the rise of the BLT — including when the abbreviation first came into use — aren't set in stone. As is the case with many great recipes, this is one that evolved over time.

But there are a few things we know to be true:

16TH CEN. — Tomatoes are introduced to Europe.

18TH CEN. — Mayonnaise is invented in France.

1903 — *Good Housekeeping Everyday Cook Book* publishes a recipe for a club sandwich, which included bacon, lettuce, and tomato, along with mayo and a slice of turkey. (One of the earliest mentions of something resembling a BLT.)

1940s — BLTs become popular following WWII thanks to the rise of supermarkets, meaning fresh tomatoes and lettuce are available year round.

1958 — Hellman's Mayonnaise advertises their product as "traditional on bacon, lettuce, and tomato sandwiches."

2011 — The world's largest BLT is created during Iron Barley's seventh annual Tomato Fest in St. Louis, Missouri. It was 224 feet long and 18 inches wide and contained 600 pounds of bacon, 550 pounds of tomatoes, 220 heads of lettuce, and 440 pounds of bread!

WE DARE YOU!

A BLT is great on its own, but a sandwich savant like you is probably ready to take it to the next level. Think you can handle the weird, the gross, the amazing, and everything in between? Here are just a few out-there options to experiment with . . . if you dare!

CHOCOLATE CHIP COOKIE

BUFFALO SAUCE

MAC & CHEESE

MARSHMALLOW FLUFF

PEANUT BUTTER

FRIED EGG

FRENCH FRIES

MASHED POTATOES

JALAPEÑOS

RADISHES

PB&B (PEANUT BUTTER & BANANA)

Served warm and sometimes called an "Elvis Sandwich" or simply the "Elvis," the PB&B uses toasted bread, peanut butter, and mashed or sliced bananas, depending on your personal preference. You can also add honey to take your sandwich to the sweeter side, or add bacon . . . if you dare! No matter what your modifications, the PB&B is a great source of protein and potassium — perfect for days you have a big test at school or a big game after.

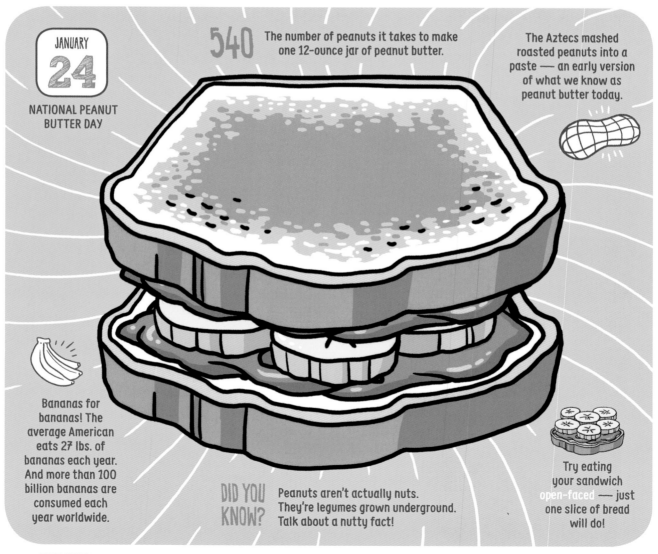

JANUARY 24

NATIONAL PEANUT BUTTER DAY

540 The number of peanuts it takes to make one 12-ounce jar of peanut butter.

The Aztecs mashed roasted peanuts into a paste — an early version of what we know as peanut butter today.

Bananas for bananas! The average American eats 27 lbs. of bananas each year. And more than 100 billion bananas are consumed each year worldwide.

DID YOU KNOW? Peanuts aren't actually nuts. They're legumes grown underground. Talk about a nutty fact!

Try eating your sandwich open-faced — just one slice of bread will do!

WHITE BREAD

PEANUT BUTTER

SLICED BANANAS

PEANUT BUTTER

WHITE BREAD

A SANDWICH FIT FOR
THE KING!

Rumor has it that Elvis ate his PB&B with bacon as well — and could eat 12–15 sandwiches in a single sitting!

Add a drizzle of honey for extra sweetness!

Try banana bread for additional banana-y-ness!

PB&B (PEANUT BUTTER & BANANA)

CHICKEN — AND — WAFFLES

Is it breakfast? Is it lunch? Who knows! We don't have all the answers — all we know is that it's delicious. This southern staple is equal parts sweet and savory; and the nooks and crannies in the waffle — perfect for capturing cheese or maple syrup — don't hurt either. Chicken and waffles, a match made in culinary heaven!

1789

Thomas Jefferson purchases and brings a French waffle iron to the United States.

1964

The Belgian waffle is introduced to America at the World's Fair.

17TH CENTURY

Chicken and waffles are first paired in Pennsylvania Dutch country. This version used pulled chicken and gravy on top of waffles.

Waffles originated in the Middle Ages when bakeries started creating communion wafers for churches.

1938

Wells Supper Club in Harlem, New York, opens and creates a new version of chicken and waffles — still famous today! — for musicians who arrived too late for dinner but too early for breakfast.

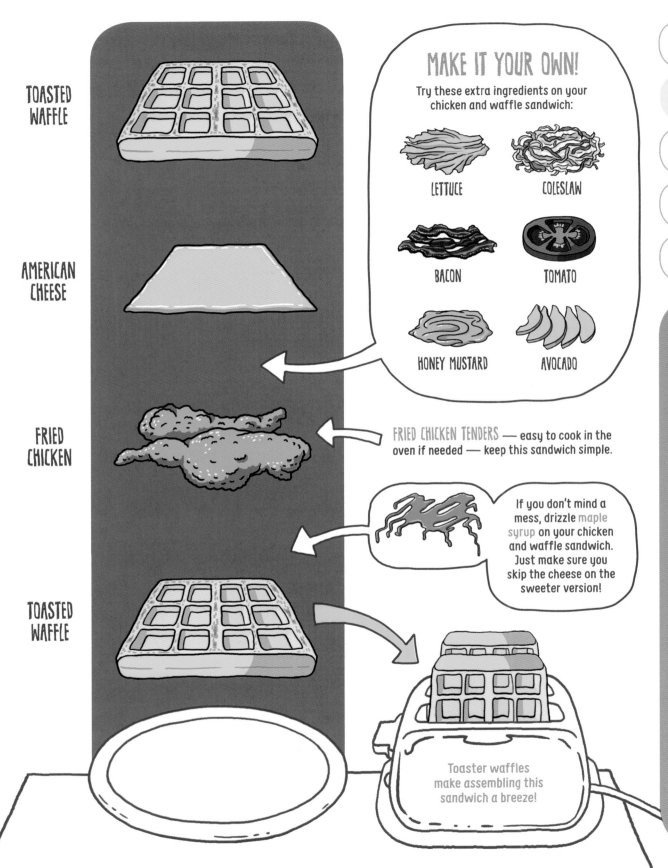

TOASTED WAFFLE

AMERICAN CHEESE

FRIED CHICKEN

TOASTED WAFFLE

MAKE IT YOUR OWN!

Try these extra ingredients on your chicken and waffle sandwich:

LETTUCE

COLESLAW

BACON

TOMATO

HONEY MUSTARD

AVOCADO

FRIED CHICKEN TENDERS — easy to cook in the oven if needed — keep this sandwich simple.

If you don't mind a mess, drizzle maple syrup on your chicken and waffle sandwich. Just make sure you skip the cheese on the sweeter version!

Toaster waffles make assembling this sandwich a breeze!

CHICKEN AND WAFFLES

CLUB

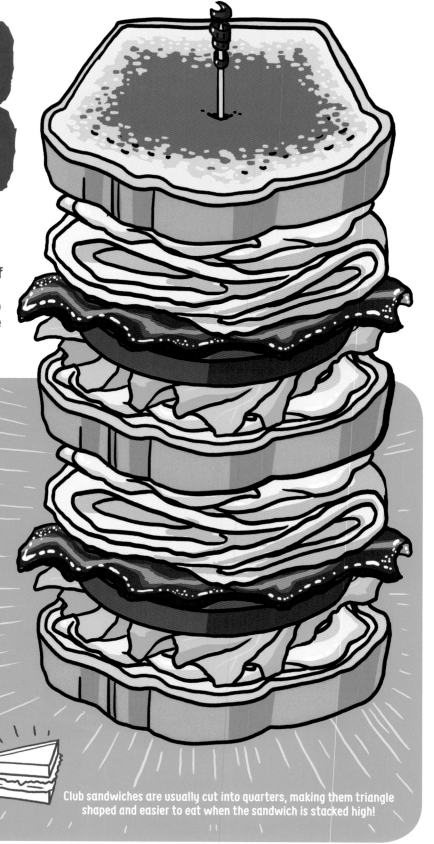

Stack your BLT sky high and toss on some turkey and you've got yourself a club sandwich. This tall sandwich is a real mouthful — layers upon layers of toasty bread, crisp bacon, and savory turkey, plus lettuce, tomato, and mayo stack up to create the classic club. The only limit is how much sandwich you can fit in your mouth in one bite.

1894

The year the club sandwich is rumored to have been created at the Saratoga Club House, a gambling establishment in Saratoga Springs, New York.

The club sandwich has a more formal name too — the clubhouse sandwich.

1903

The first recipe for a club sandwich appears in the *Good Housekeeping Everyday Cook Book*.

Club sandwiches are usually cut into quarters, making them triangle shaped and easier to eat when the sandwich is stacked high!

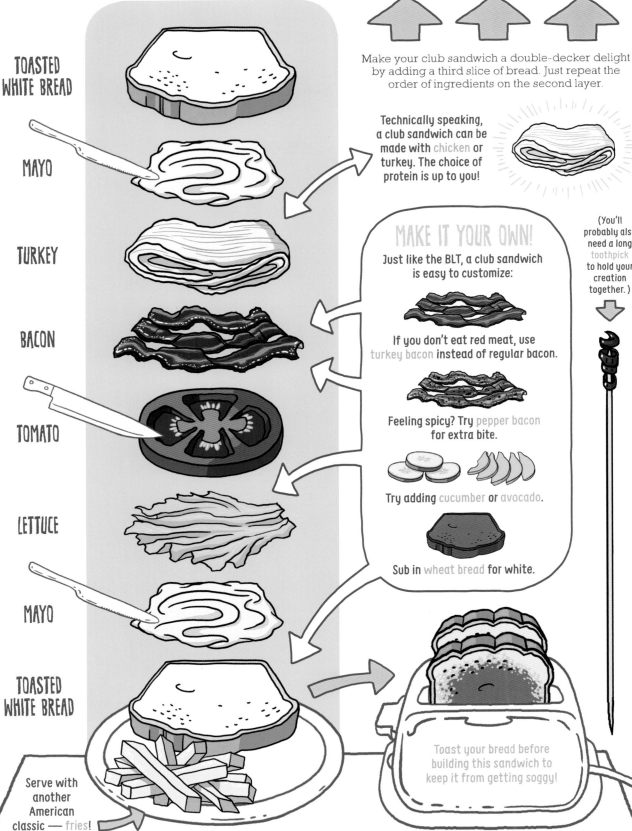

TOASTED WHITE BREAD

MAYO

TURKEY

BACON

TOMATO

LETTUCE

MAYO

TOASTED WHITE BREAD

Serve with another American classic — fries!

Make your club sandwich a double-decker delight by adding a third slice of bread. Just repeat the order of ingredients on the second layer.

Technically speaking, a club sandwich can be made with chicken or turkey. The choice of protein is up to you!

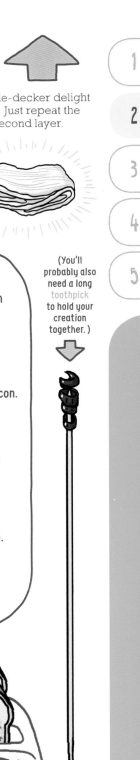

MAKE IT YOUR OWN!

Just like the BLT, a club sandwich is easy to customize:

If you don't eat red meat, use turkey bacon instead of regular bacon.

Feeling spicy? Try pepper bacon for extra bite.

Try adding cucumber or avocado.

Sub in wheat bread for white.

(You'll probably also need a long toothpick to hold your creation together.)

Toast your bread before building this sandwich to keep it from getting soggy!

BAGEL AND LOX

Biting into a soft, chewy bagel in the morning is the ultimate delight. Smear on some cream cheese, add some lox, salty capers, tomato, and red onion, and you've got yourself a real breakfast sandwich! You can serve this sandwich open-faced, as is traditional, or put the top on if you prefer your bagel and lox with a lid. Feeling extra hungry? Use both halves of the bagel as their own individual sandwiches.

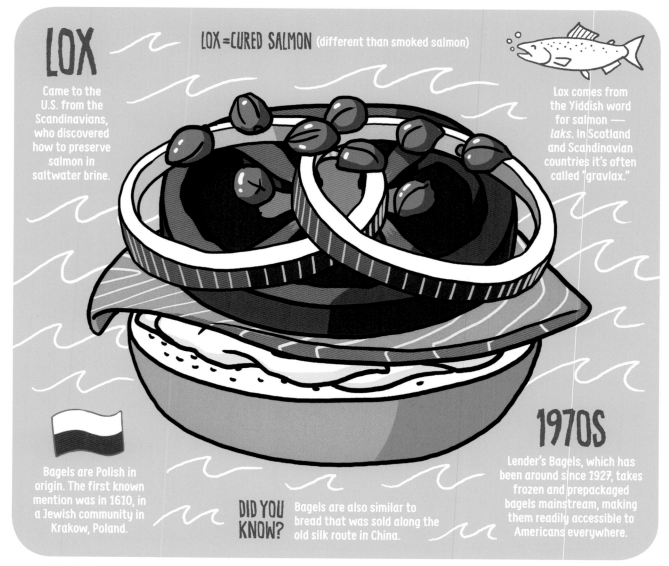

LOX

LOX = CURED SALMON (different than smoked salmon)

Came to the U.S. from the Scandinavians, who discovered how to preserve salmon in saltwater brine.

Lox comes from the Yiddish word for salmon — *laks*. In Scotland and Scandinavian countries it's often called "gravlax."

Bagels are Polish in origin. The first known mention was in 1610, in a Jewish community in Krakow, Poland.

DID YOU KNOW? Bagels are also similar to bread that was sold along the old silk route in China.

1970S

Lender's Bagels, which has been around since 1927, takes frozen and prepackaged bagels mainstream, making them readily accessible to Americans everywhere.

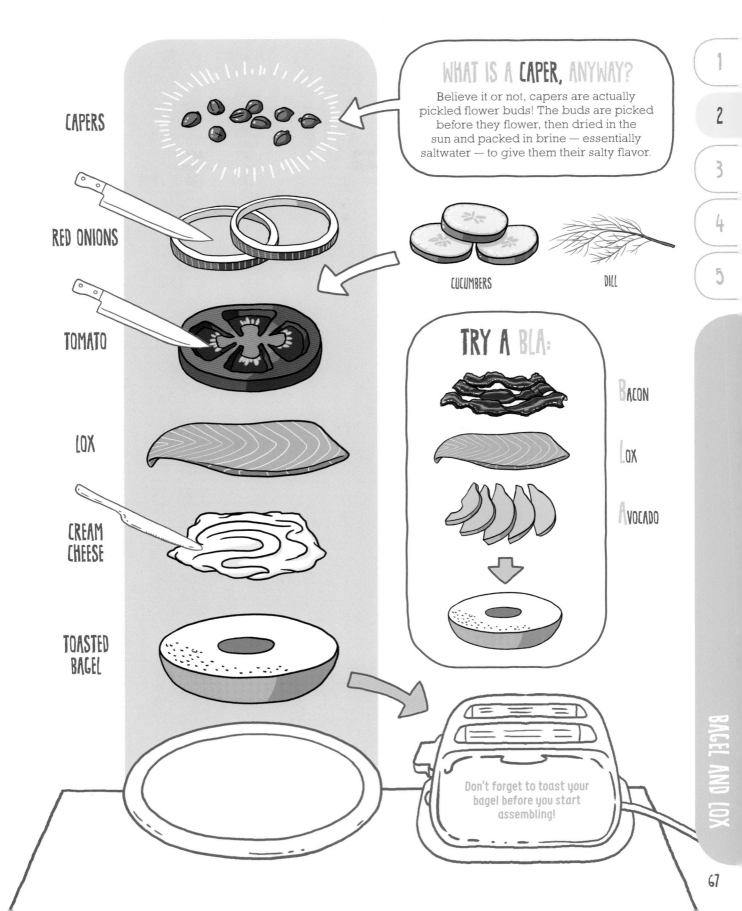

CAPERS

RED ONIONS

TOMATO

LOX

CREAM CHEESE

TOASTED BAGEL

WHAT IS A **CAPER**, ANYWAY?

Believe it or not, capers are actually pickled flower buds! The buds are picked before they flower, then dried in the sun and packed in brine — essentially saltwater — to give them their salty flavor.

CUCUMBERS

DILL

TRY A **BLA**:

BACON

LOX

AVOCADO

Don't forget to toast your bagel before you start assembling!

BAGEL AND LOX

LEVEL 3

OVEN/BROILER

Well, well, well . . . look at you! Moving right along to Level 3! In this section you'll be creating sandwiches that require the use of another major kitchen appliance — the oven. Some might be baked and others might use the broiler (that top rack in the oven closest to the top) to melt cheese.

Before you start using the oven or broiler, check with an adult to make sure you have permission. Once you do, here are a few rules to follow:

Learn how to use the oven. Have an adult show you how the oven in your kitchen works.

Always use hot pads or oven mitts when removing something from the oven. The plate or dish will be extremely hot, even if it's only been in there for a short time.

Use the oven light to check on food rather than opening the oven door. (You don't want the heat to escape!)

Keep an extra-close watch on food under the broiler. Because it's so close to the heat, it will cook quickly and can burn if you're not paying close attention. (Try setting a timer for 2–3 minutes so you don't forget!)

A convection oven cooks food faster because it circulates hot air around the oven, cooking more evenly. If you're using a convection oven, a good rule of thumb is to lower your cooking temperature by 25 degrees. (You can also keep the temperature the same and check your food about three-quarters of the way through the cooking time.)

Don't leave food in the oven unattended.

Make sure to turn the oven off when you're done using it.

SPAGHETTI

Let's face it — some foods are just better eaten the next day. That's the beauty of this delicious — and admittedly messy — spaghetti sandwich. You don't have to worry about whipping up a fresh batch of pasta for this one. Just open the fridge, find those leftover noodles, then add tomato sauce, cheese, and garlic bread to create a handheld Italian feast!

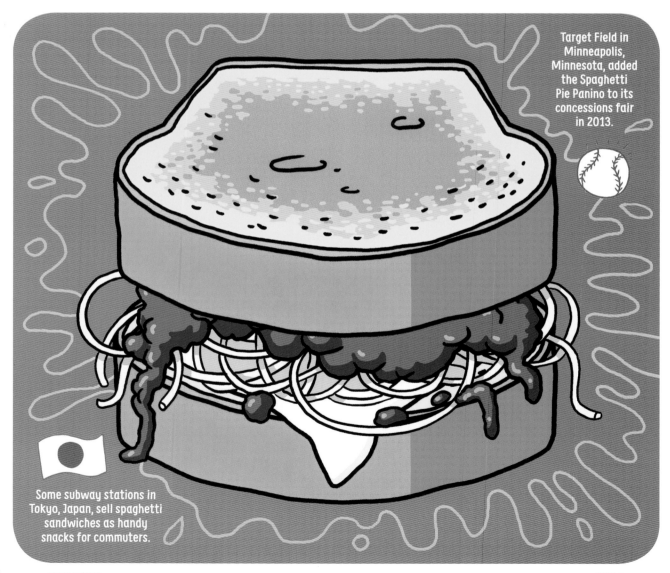

Target Field in Minneapolis, Minnesota, added the Spaghetti Pie Panino to its concessions fair in 2013.

Some subway stations in Tokyo, Japan, sell spaghetti sandwiches as handy snacks for commuters.

OVEN-
TOASTED
GARLIC
BREAD

Don't forget to butter both slices of bread, and feel free to add parmesan, garlic powder, or oregano for extra flavor!

TOMATO
SAUCE

This spaghetti sandwich is vegetarian, but you can just as easily use sauce with ground meat in it.

SPAGHETTI

Swap the tomato sauce for pesto!

MOZZARELLA
CHEESE

Leftover spaghetti can be used and eaten hot or cold.

OVEN-
TOASTED
GARLIC
BREAD

Try it on a hot dog bun!

Bake your garlic toast for a few minutes to get it warm, toasty, and crunchy!

BAKE   350°   TIMER
                10:00

Try it with

SIDE SALAD   SPARKLING WATER

SPAGHETTI

MEATBALL SUB

Not sure what to do with those leftover meatballs from dinner? Grab a hoagie roll, some extra cheese, and turn the whole thing into a sandwich, of course! It might be messy, but it'll also be delicious. Pile all your ingredients onto a sliced roll, and ask an adult to help you stick it under the broiler until the cheese is nice and bubbly. Then enjoy eating! You won't need any help for that.

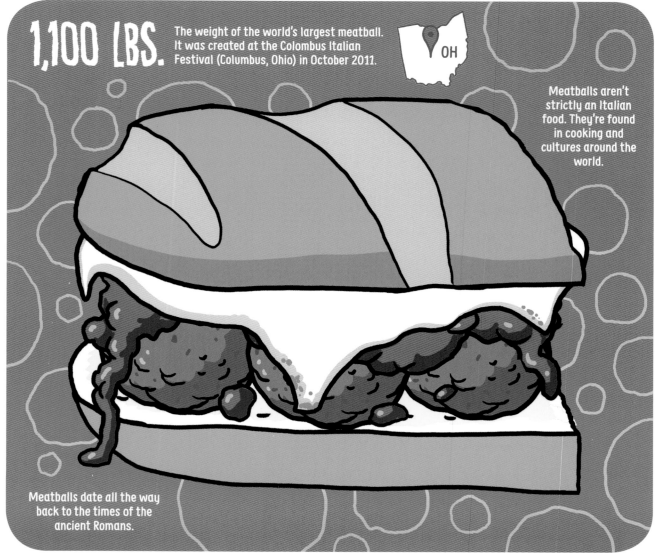

1,100 LBS. The weight of the world's largest meatball. It was created at the Colombus Italian Festival (Columbus, Ohio) in October 2011.

OH

Meatballs aren't strictly an Italian food. They're found in cooking and cultures around the world.

Meatballs date all the way back to the times of the ancient Romans.

HOAGIE ROLL

MOZZARELLA CHEESE

MARINARA SAUCE

MEATBALLS

HOAGIE ROLL

You can make meatball sliders using the same fillings with smaller rolls/buns.

Add parmesan to make your sub extra cheesy!

No leftovers? No problem! Frozen meatballs work just as well as leftovers.

CUSTOMIZE IT!

Meatballs are often made with a mixture of ground beef, pork, or sausage, but you can just as easily use ground turkey or chicken instead (poultry makes meatballs even more moist!).

Once you've assembled your sammie (minus the top), a few minutes under the broiler in the oven will do the trick!

TIMER 2:50   BROIL   HI

Try it with

SIDE SALAD

COLA

FRIED FISH

The fried fish sandwich can be found from the Atlantic to the Pacific in the U.S., and why not?! It's easy, delicious, and satisfying. You can use oven-baked fried fish fillets as the meat in this sandwich. Just have an adult help you with the oven, and follow the cooking instructions on the package. Walleye, cod, and halibut are great choices for fish, but any type of fried whitefish will do.

23% of all Filet-O-Fish sandwiches are sold during Lent.

1962 The Filet-O-Fish is invented by Lou Groen, a McDonald's franchise owner in Cincinnati, Ohio. He created it to remedy his store's slow sales on Fridays during Lent, when most Catholics abstain from meat.

300 MIL. The number of Filet-O-Fish sandwiches McDonald's sells each year.

The original Filet-O-Fish cost only $0.29 when it was added to McDonald's permanent menu in 1965.

2,324 The number of sandwiches sold in the first month the Filet-O-Fish was on McDonald's menu.

HOAGIE ROLL

TARTAR SAUCE

COLESLAW

FRIED FISH FILLET

TARTAR SAUCE

HOAGIE ROLL

Swap out the hoagie for a hamburger bun — or use whatever bread fits the size of your fish fillet best.

HAMBURGER BUN

HOT DOG BUN

MULTI-GRAIN BREAD

ITALIAN ROLL

Tartar sauce first began appearing in cookbooks in the 19th century and originated in eastern France. The name comes from the French sauce *tartare*. Modern versions are mayonnaise based and include pickle relish, onions, capers, chives, and parsley.

Use any frozen whitefish for your fried fish sandwich — follow the cooking instructions on the package.

No fish fillet on hand? Feel free to use fish sticks instead!

BAKE | 350° | TIMER 25:00

Serve with French fries, just like fish and chips!

CHICKEN PARMESAN SLIDERS

Why eat one sandwich when you could eat multiple mini sandwiches? That's the beauty of sliders. The same full-sized sandwich you love shrunk down to nearly bite-sized. Sliders are perfect for a party or to enjoy on your own. And while you *could* make just one, why would you? We suggest prepping a pan of these sliders so you can eat — or share — as many as you'd like. (Just remember, most mouths have a one-slider-at-a-time limit.)

1921 The year White Castle, home of Slyders, first opened in Wichita, Kansas.

5¢ The original cost of a slider at White Castle.

What came first, the chicken or the egg(plant)? Chicken parmesan is actually a variation of eggplant parmesan, an Italian dish that originated in Sicily.

WHAT'S IN A NAME?

No one is entirely sure how sliders got theirs, but it likely has to do with how they slid across the griddle back in the day, or how easily they slide down when you're eating a few.

SLIDER BUN

Brush the top with melted butter, then dust with garlic powder and Italian seasoning.

PARMESAN CHEESE

Chicken Parmesan Sliders are just one option — you can use this same method to make any other type of slider as well! Try pulled pork or chicken sliders, or cheeseburger sliders.

MOZZARELLA CHEESE

MARINARA SAUCE

CHICKEN TENDER

If you don't want fried chicken, substitute leftover chicken breast or rotisserie chicken.

SLIDER BUN

Assemble the bottom half of your slider (up to the mozzarella) and have an adult help you put it under the broiler to melt the cheese.

OR!

Ready to make your sliders in bulk? With a grownup's help, preheat the oven to 375 degrees. Cut your slider buns in half and place the bottom halves in a baking dish or tray. Layer on all your ingredients and place the half of your slider buns on top. Brush on melted butter, garlic, and seasonings, and bake for 20 minutes.

TIMER 2:50 BROIL HI

Then top it with parmesan and the top bun.

LEVEL 4

STOVE, SKILLET & PANINI PRESS

You're almost there . . . Level 4 awaits! In this section, you'll be tackling hot sandwiches made on the stove (usually in a skillet) or on a panini press. Before you start cooking with gas (or electric or induction, as the case may be) have an adult show you how to work your stove. Every stove is different, and it's important to know and understand the controls, heat levels, and other features before you begin.

Once your stove tutorial is complete, use these general tips to keep you and your sandwiches safe in the kitchen:

Use a skillet or pan large enough to fit your sandwich. You'll also want to make sure you have room to flip it using a spatula.

Turn the handles for all pots and pans toward the back when you're cooking. That way you're less likely to bump or knock into them, creating a kitchen catastrophe and a safety hazard.

A nonstick skillet works best for grilled sandwiches. We also recommend buttering the outside of the bread so it doesn't stick to the pan during grilling.

Never pour water on a grease fire. Instead, quickly cover the pan with a lid and get help from an adult.

Never leave something unattended on the stove — and don't get distracted. Your sandwich and skillet should have your full attention.

It's a good idea to have a fire extinguisher in or near the kitchen, just in case of emergency. (Know how to use it.)

Use pot holders when taking something off the stove. Handles can get hot as well.

Always turn the stove off when you're done using it.

GRILLED CHEESE

There's no better comfort food than bread and cheese — and grilled? Well that's just taking it to the next level. This classic sandwich can be made on the stove, in the oven, or using a panini press if you want to get extra fancy. Try experimenting with different types of cheese, and pair your sandwich with tomato soup for the ultimate comfort-food meal.

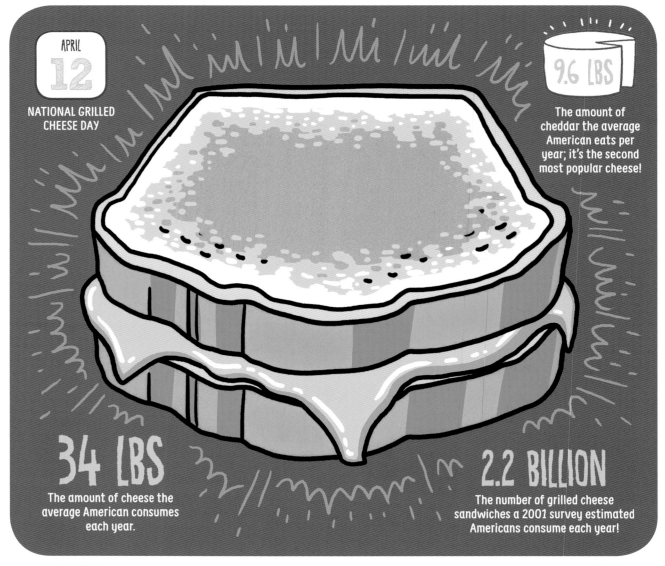

APRIL
12

NATIONAL GRILLED
CHEESE DAY

9.6 LBS

The amount of
cheddar the average
American eats per
year; it's the second
most popular cheese!

34 LBS

The amount of cheese the
average American consumes
each year.

2.2 BILLION

The number of grilled cheese
sandwiches a 2001 survey estimated
Americans consume each year!

WHITE BREAD

Don't forget to butter the outside of both slices of bread before grilling — that's crucial to get the outside of your sandwich nice and crispy!

The Brits do it differently — the cheese-and-pickle sandwich is popular across the pond! It's not usually toasted, but we say give it a try!

AMERICAN CHEESE

Use Texas toast for an extra-thick grilled cheese.

Try multi-grain bread for extra crunch and nuttiness.

WHITE BREAD

Use mayo in place of butter for grilling.

Grill your sandwich for a couple minutes on each side, until the bread is golden-brown and the cheese is melted.

Try it with

TOMATO SOUP

MILK

MORE GRILLED CHEESE ON PGS. 82–83

GRILLED CHEESE

THE HISTORY OF THE GRILLED CHEESE

Cooked bread and cheese has been popular since ancient times, but the modern grilled cheese, now a staple in homes across the country — and one of the best comfort foods around! — didn't get its start until much later.

Journey with us down the grilled-cheese timeline:

1920s — Inexpensive sliced bread and American cheese are made available to the masses. (Cheese sandwiches at this time are mostly served open faced, with one slice of bread and grated American cheese.)

1930s — During the Great Depression, the "cheese dream" (an open-faced grilled cheese sandwich) becomes increasingly popular as an easy, inexpensive way to feed friends and family during Sunday supper.

1940s — During WWII, Navy cooks make countless grilled cheese sandwiches, as instructed by official government-issued cookbooks.

1949 — Kraft singles are introduced.

1960s — "Grilled cheese" finally makes an appearance in print. Before this, these sandwiches were mostly known as "toasted cheese" or "melted cheese" sandwiches.

1965 — Supermarkets start stocking Kraft singles; this is around the same time the second slice of bread was added to the grilled cheese, making it a more filling meal.

WE DARE YOU!

A grilled cheese is great on its own, but a sandwich savant like you is probably ready to take it to the next level. Think you can handle the weird, the gross, the amazing, and everything in between? Here are just a few out-there options to experiment with . . . if you dare!

APPLE PIE FILLING

HOT SAUCE

SPICY PICKLES

CRUNCHY PEANUT BUTTER

HONEY

APRICOT JELLY

GRAVY

POTATO CHIPS

RANCH DRESSING

BANANAS

MAC AND CHEESE

Macaroni and cheese is great fresh — but what do you do with that day-old stuff? Reheated mac and cheese is never quite as good as the original . . . right? Think again! This mac and cheese sandwich is made with leftovers in mind! Grab some cold mac and cheese from the fridge, sandwich it between some bread, grill it up, and you're good to go! (Cold leftover mac works best since it will hold its shape better — perfect for a grilled sandwich!)

1937
Kraft introduced its boxed version of macaroni and cheese.

CHEDDAR The most popular cheese used in macaroni and cheese.

8 MILLION
The number of boxes of Kraft macaroni and cheese sold the first year it was introduced.

10 MONTHS
The shelf life of a box of Kraft mac and cheese.

Macaroni and cheese has Italian origins — recipes appear as far back as the 13th century in southern Italy.

Macaroni pudding — the long ago name for mac and cheese in Connecticut.

1 MILLION
The number of boxes of Kraft mac and cheese now sold daily. Talk about a mac attack!

WHITE
BREAD

AMERICAN
CHEESE

MAC AND
CHEESE

WHITE
BREAD

Don't forget to butter the outside of both slices of bread before grilling — that's crucial to get the outside of your sandwich nice and crispy!

Try using Texas toast or garlic bread in place of white bread for a heartier sandwich.

Make your mac and cheese sandwich your own by adding tomato and/or bacon! (Use turkey bacon if you don't eat red meat.)

Grill your sandwich for a couple minutes on each side, until the bread is golden-brown and the cheese is melted.

RUMOR HAS IT . . .

Thomas Jefferson, one of America's founding fathers, might also be the man behind mac and cheese in the states. While visiting France and Italy, Jefferson fell in love with macaroni. He enjoyed the dish so much that he arranged to bring noodle recipes and a pasta machine back to America. (He later had both macaroni and parmesan cheese imported to use at his home, Monticello.) Jefferson even served mac and cheese at a state dinner in 1802, during his term as president.

(Jefferson was hardly the first to invent macaroni and cheese, though — the earliest known recipe was written down in 1769.)

MAC AND CHEESE

HAM AND PINEAPPLE

Ham and pineapple aren't just pizza toppings anymore — this Hawaiian-inspired combo is also scrumptious on a sandwich! The sweet juice of pineapple perfectly complements the savory taste of ham, and you can never go wrong when you add cheese to the mix. Grill the whole thing up until the bread is golden, the cheese is melty, and the ham is hot, and then dig in!

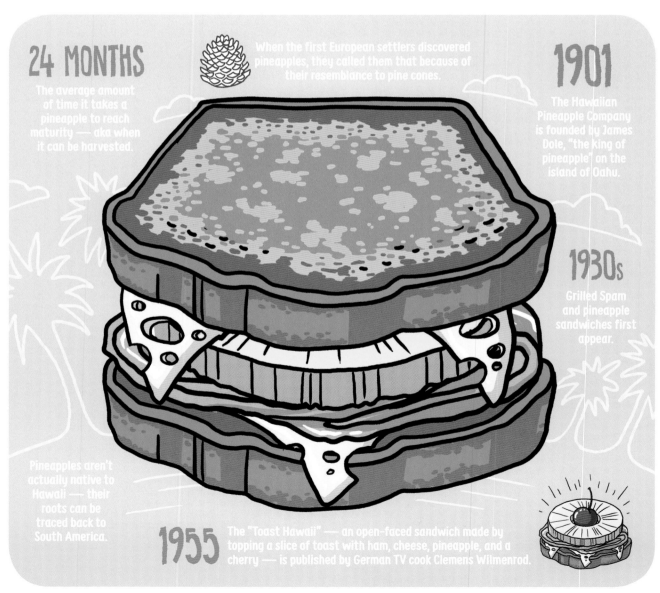

24 MONTHS
The average amount of time it takes a pineapple to reach maturity — aka when it can be harvested.

When the first European settlers discovered pineapples, they called them that because of their resemblance to pine cones.

1901
The Hawaiian Pineapple Company is founded by James Dole, "the king of pineapple" on the island of Oahu.

1930s
Grilled Spam and pineapple sandwiches first appear.

Pineapples aren't actually native to Hawaii — their roots can be traced back to South America.

1955
The "Toast Hawaii" — an open-faced sandwich made by topping a slice of toast with ham, cheese, pineapple, and a cherry — is published by German TV cook Clemens Wilmenrod.

WHEAT BREAD

SWISS CHEESE

PINEAPPLE

HAM

SWISS CHEESE

WHEAT BREAD

Don't forget to butter the outside of both slices of bread before grilling!

Swap out the Swiss for mozzarella, add tomato sauce, and make your ham and pineapple a modified pizza sandwich!

Fresh or canned pineapple both work — use whatever you have on hand!

Grill your sandwich for a couple minutes on each side, until the bread is golden-brown and the cheese is melted.

If you have a panini press you can use that in place of a skillet or grill pan.

HAM AND PINEAPPLE

S'MORE

Ready for s'more sandwiches? You don't need summer, or a bonfire, or marshmallow-roasting sticks to enjoy this sweet treat. You can whip up this campfire-inspired sandwich in the comfort of your own kitchen, no open flame required. Just be prepared to make extra, because we can almost guarantee everyone will want s'more.

1927
The first published recipe for "Some More" appears in *Tramping and Trailing with the Girl Scouts.*

90
Americans buy 90 million pounds of marshmallows a year — the equivalent of approximately 1,300 gray whales.

AUGUST 10
NATIONAL S'MORES DAY

A "Graham Cracker Sandwich" recipe appeared as early as 1920. At that time it was already popular with Boy Scouts and Girl Scouts.

423
The Guinness World Record for the most people making s'mores at one time. The record was set in Huntington Beach, California, on April 21, 2016.

1938
The contraction "s'more" first appears — it's in a publication aimed at summer camps.

WHITE BREAD

GRAHAM CRACKER CRUMBS

MARSHMALLOW FLUFF

CHOCOLATE

WHITE BREAD

PRO TIP!

Butter both sides of the bread before grilling. Feeling fancy? Try dipping the butter side of the bread in graham cracker crumbs before grilling it for a more authentic tasting s'more.

You can use real marshmallows, but we recommend using marshmallow fluff or creme — it will melt and warm up much faster.

Use Nutella in place of chocolate for a different flavor.

Try adding peanut butter to take your s'mores sandwich up an extra notch.

Grill your sandwich for a couple minutes on each side, until the bread is golden-brown and the toppings are gooey.

Try it with a hot dog — a great camping companion for your sweet campfire treat!

PIZZA MELT

What's better than pizza? Trick question — nothing is better than pizza! Well, unless you count this pizza sandwich, this is. A culinary masterpiece that combines the best of both worlds — pizza and sandwiches — this ooey, gooey, cheesy creation can be personalized any way you like. Our version includes the classic combo of pepperoni and mozzarella, but feel free to substitute another meat, or opt for veggies to lighten up your sandwich a bit. Just don't skimp on the cheese!

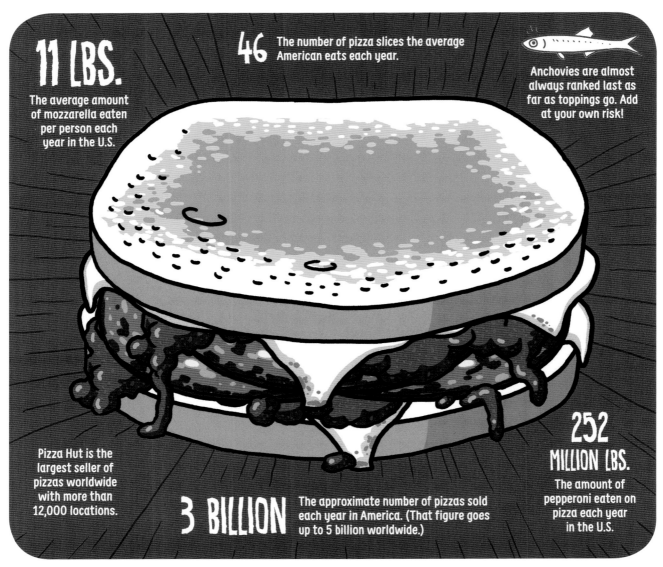

11 LBS.
The average amount of mozzarella eaten per person each year in the U.S.

46 The number of pizza slices the average American eats each year.

Anchovies are almost always ranked last as far as toppings go. Add at your own risk!

Pizza Hut is the largest seller of pizzas worldwide with more than 12,000 locations.

3 BILLION The approximate number of pizzas sold each year in America. (That figure goes up to 5 billion worldwide.)

252 MILLION LBS.
The amount of pepperoni eaten on pizza each year in the U.S.

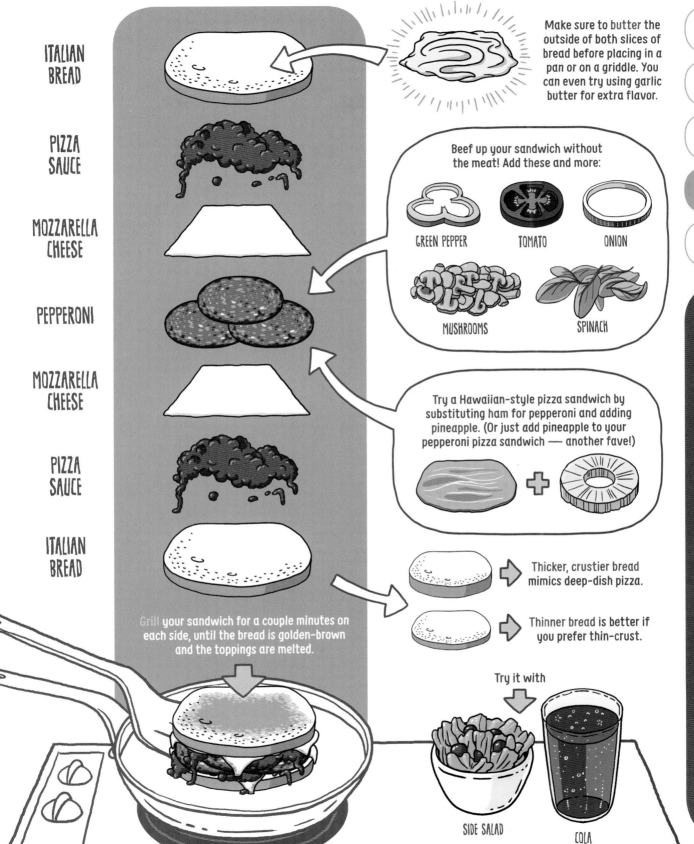

ITALIAN BREAD

PIZZA SAUCE

MOZZARELLA CHEESE

PEPPERONI

MOZZARELLA CHEESE

PIZZA SAUCE

ITALIAN BREAD

Make sure to butter the outside of both slices of bread before placing in a pan or on a griddle. You can even try using garlic butter for extra flavor.

Beef up your sandwich without the meat! Add these and more:

GREEN PEPPER

TOMATO

ONION

MUSHROOMS

SPINACH

Try a Hawaiian-style pizza sandwich by substituting ham for pepperoni and adding pineapple. (Or just add pineapple to your pepperoni pizza sandwich — another fave!)

Thicker, crustier bread mimics deep-dish pizza.

Thinner bread is better if you prefer thin-crust.

Grill your sandwich for a couple minutes on each side, until the bread is golden-brown and the toppings are melted.

Try it with

SIDE SALAD

COLA

PIZZA MELT

NUTELLA AND BANANA

Are there any two items that pair together better than Nutella and bananas? (Well, maybe peanut butter and jelly, but that's a different story and a different sandwich.) This rich, creamy hazelnut-cocoa spread is best served warm, so we recommend grilling up this sandwich on the stove. Serve with an ice-cold glass of milk to wash it all down!

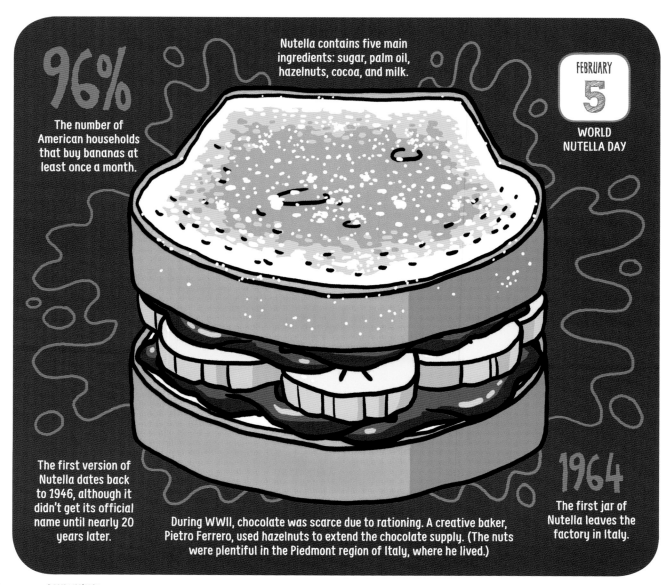

96%
The number of American households that buy bananas at least once a month.

Nutella contains five main ingredients: sugar, palm oil, hazelnuts, cocoa, and milk.

FEBRUARY
5
WORLD NUTELLA DAY

The first version of Nutella dates back to 1946, although it didn't get its official name until nearly 20 years later.

During WWII, chocolate was scarce due to rationing. A creative baker, Pietro Ferrero, used hazelnuts to extend the chocolate supply. (The nuts were plentiful in the Piedmont region of Italy, where he lived.)

1964
The first jar of Nutella leaves the factory in Italy.

FRENCH BREAD/CROISSANT

Don't forget to butter the outside of your bread before grilling! (This will only work on flat bread, not a croissant.)

NUTELLA

SLICED BANANAS

NUTELLA

FRENCH BREAD/CROISSANT

BANANA SPLIT!

Try adding the following ingredients to your ooey, gooey sandwich to make it even more delicious:

PEANUT BUTTER

STRAWBERRIES

PINEAPPLE JELLY

HONEY

CINNAMON

SHREDDED COCONUT

Grill your sandwich for a couple minutes on each side, until the bread is golden-brown and the toppings are gooey.

Dust your sandwich with powdered sugar before eating.

ULTIMATE GRILLED CHEESE

Ready to take the cheese factor to the next level? The ULTIMATE grilled cheese piles on not one, not two, not three or four — but FIVE types of cheese. That's five layers of gooey, creamy goodness. Prepare your palette, because this is one sandwich not for the faint of heart.

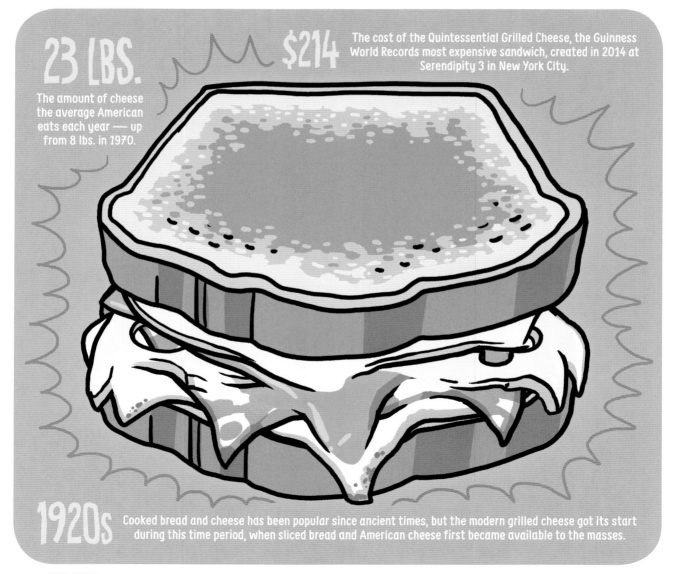

23 LBS.
The amount of cheese the average American eats each year — up from 8 lbs. in 1970.

$214
The cost of the Quintessential Grilled Cheese, the Guinness World Records most expensive sandwich, created in 2014 at Serendipity 3 in New York City.

1920s
Cooked bread and cheese has been popular since ancient times, but the modern grilled cheese got its start during this time period, when sliced bread and American cheese first became available to the masses.

SOURDOUGH BREAD

Don't forget to butter the bread before grilling! Add garlic salt to your sandwich for extra pizazz.

PROVOLONE CHEESE

CHEDDAR CHEESE

CUSTOMIZE IT!

Try swapping out any of these cheeses for some of your other favorites:

SWISS CHEESE

PEPPER JACK

BRIE

GOUDA

COLBY-JACK CHEESE

MUENSTER

MOZZARELLA CHEESE

HAVARTI

AMERICAN

SOURDOUGH BREAD

Grill your sandwich for a couple minutes on each side, until the bread is golden-brown and the toppings are gooey.

Try it with

TOMATO SOUP

MILK

ULTIMATE GRILLED CHEESE

CHICKEN APPLE BRIE

Warm, melty brie and tart, crunchy apples — is there any better combination? Just add some savory chicken, and press the whole shebang in a panini press, and you've got yourself a sandwich! You don't have to be a celebrity chef to whip up this creation either. Leftover rotisserie chicken or sliced deli meat work just fine. Make sure to thinly slice your apples before laying them on so they'll get warm along with everything else.

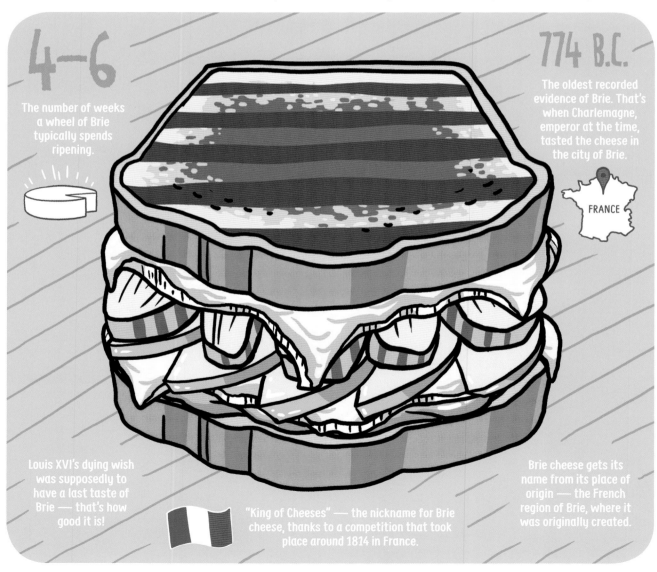

4-6
The number of weeks a wheel of Brie typically spends ripening.

774 B.C.
The oldest recorded evidence of Brie. That's when Charlemagne, emperor at the time, tasted the cheese in the city of Brie.

FRANCE

Louis XVI's dying wish was supposedly to have a last taste of Brie — that's how good it is!

"King of Cheeses" — the nickname for Brie cheese, thanks to a competition that took place around 1814 in France.

Brie cheese gets its name from its place of origin — the French region of Brie, where it was originally created.

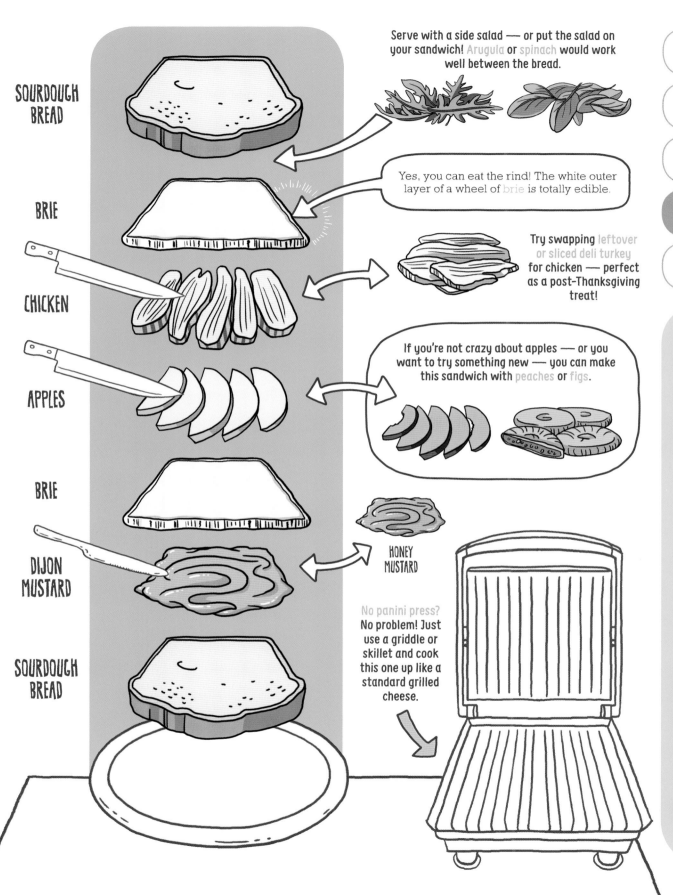

SOURDOUGH BREAD

Serve with a side salad — or put the salad on your sandwich! Arugula or spinach would work well between the bread.

BRIE

Yes, you can eat the rind! The white outer layer of a wheel of brie is totally edible.

CHICKEN

Try swapping leftover or sliced deli turkey for chicken — perfect as a post-Thanksgiving treat!

APPLES

If you're not crazy about apples — or you want to try something new — you can make this sandwich with peaches or figs.

BRIE

DIJON MUSTARD

HONEY MUSTARD

No panini press? No problem! Just use a griddle or skillet and cook this one up like a standard grilled cheese.

SOURDOUGH BREAD

CHICKEN APPLE BRIE

MEATLOAF

Meatloaf is a Midwestern dinner staple, and it's just as delicious the day after. All you need to whip up this tasty treat is access to leftovers! Try a cold meatloaf sandwich — soft white bread, leftover meatloaf, and a little mayo — or experiment with this hot version, complete with melty mozzarella and marinara sauce. Meatloaf, turkey loaf, and veggie loaf all work well, depending on your personal preference.

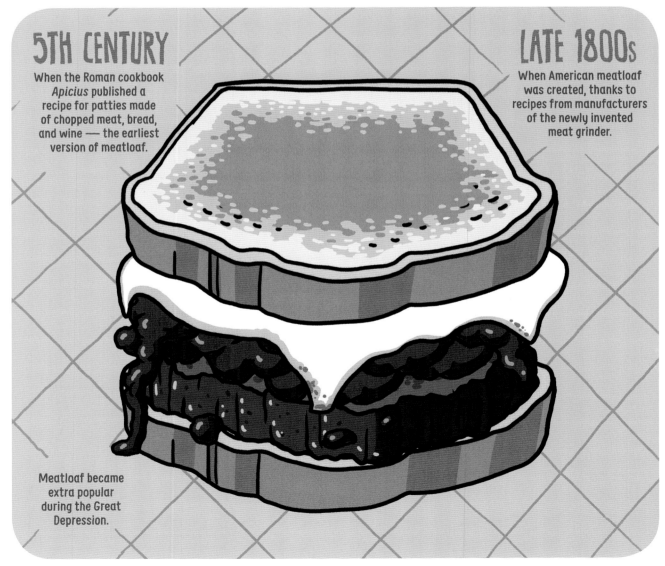

5TH CENTURY

When the Roman cookbook *Apicius* published a recipe for patties made of chopped meat, bread, and wine — the earliest version of meatloaf.

LATE 1800s

When American meatloaf was created, thanks to recipes from manufacturers of the newly invented meat grinder.

Meatloaf became extra popular during the Great Depression.

WHITE BREAD

MOZZARELLA CHEESE

MARINARA SAUCE

MEATLOAF

WHITE BREAD

Grill your sandwich for a couple minutes on each side, until the bread is golden-brown and the toppings are gooey.

Serve with mashed potatoes, just like a real meatloaf dinner! Feeling extra adventurous? Add the mashed potatoes and gravy to your sandwich!

Cranberry relish makes a meatloaf sandwich sweet.

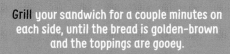

Add:

LETTUCE

TOMATO

GRILLED ONION

ARUGULA

BACON

Plain old mayo or butter on the outside help this sandwich grill up nicely! (You can also skip the grilling altogether if you'd prefer.)

MEATLOAF

ARTICHOKE =AND= CHEESE

Spinach-artichoke dip is often the hit of the party, and now it can be the star of your sandwich. The best part is, you don't need fresh artichokes to whip up this easy and delicious meal — use canned or frozen to simplify this sandwich. Then layer as much cheese as you can handle and heat up on the stove for a cheesy, delicious treat.

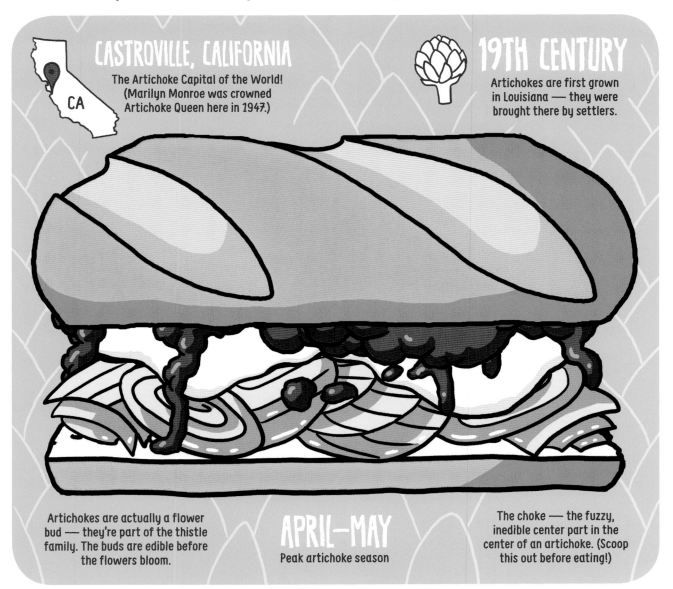

CASTROVILLE, CALIFORNIA
The Artichoke Capital of the World! (Marilyn Monroe was crowned Artichoke Queen here in 1947.)

19TH CENTURY
Artichokes are first grown in Louisiana — they were brought there by settlers.

Artichokes are actually a flower bud — they're part of the thistle family. The buds are edible before the flowers bloom.

APRIL–MAY
Peak artichoke season

The choke — the fuzzy, inedible center part in the center of an artichoke. (Scoop this out before eating!)

FRENCH BREAD

Pesto **also works well with** spinach artichoke **sandwiches!**

MARINARA SAUCE

Add parmesan **or** cream cheese **to make this sandwich even cheesier!**

PROVOLONE CHEESE

Add spinach **to create a handheld version of** spinach-artichoke dip!

ARTICHOKES

PRO TIP!

Place your artichokes on a baking sheet and pop them in a 425° oven for 15–30 minutes to roast them. Then layer them on your sandwich to help melt the cheese!

FRENCH BREAD

Or use a panini press!

ARTICHOKE AND CHEESE

PATTY MELT

Not sure what to do with the leftover burgers from your BBQ? Turn them into patty melts! Traditional patty melts are made with hamburger, but you can just as easily use a turkey burger in this uniquely American sandwich. Butter the bread and grill this one up, just like a grilled cheese. The only difference is the meat and onions in the middle!

1940s When the patty melt is said to have been invented.

Southern California is supposedly the birthplace of the patty melt.

CA

Patty Melt is also a character — a plush hamburger with a pink baseball hat and blonde braids.

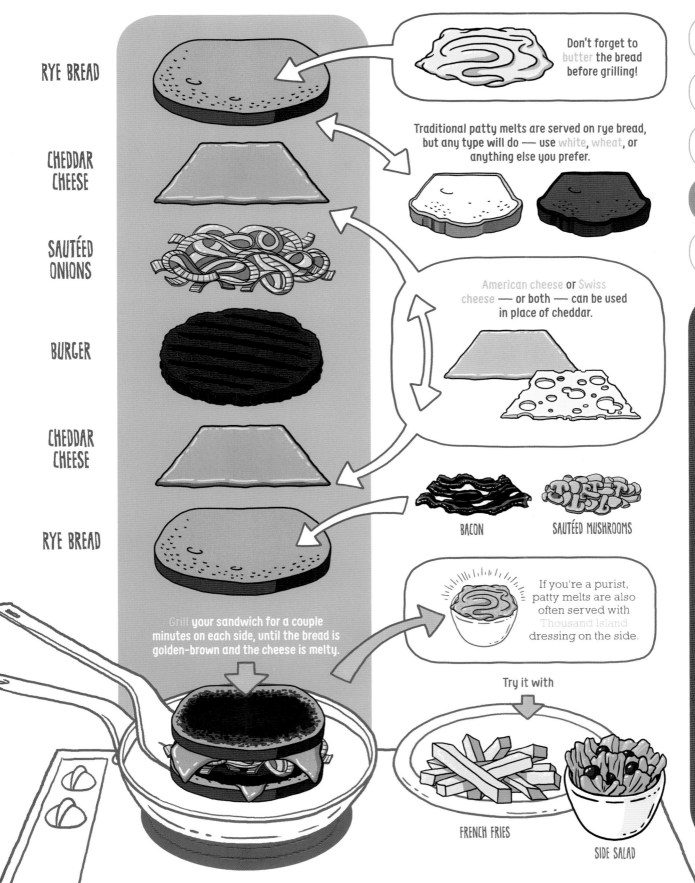

RYE BREAD

CHEDDAR CHEESE

SAUTÉED ONIONS

BURGER

CHEDDAR CHEESE

RYE BREAD

Don't forget to butter the bread before grilling!

Traditional patty melts are served on rye bread, but any type will do — use white, wheat, or anything else you prefer.

American cheese or Swiss cheese — or both — can be used in place of cheddar.

BACON

SAUTÉED MUSHROOMS

Grill your sandwich for a couple minutes on each side, until the bread is golden-brown and the cheese is melty.

If you're a purist, patty melts are also often served with Thousand Island dressing on the side.

Try it with

FRENCH FRIES

SIDE SALAD

PATTY MELT

MONTE CRISTO

A traditional Monte Cristo sandwich is fried as a whole, but let's face it — that sounds like a mess. And who needs to bust out the fryer when you have leftovers? This easy-to-make Monte Cristo features leftover French toast as the base and lid, offering the perfect sweet touch to balance savory ham, turkey, and Swiss. Heat the sandwich in a pan or on a griddle to melt the cheese and reheat the French toast, and don't forget to dust the whole thing with powdered sugar before digging in.

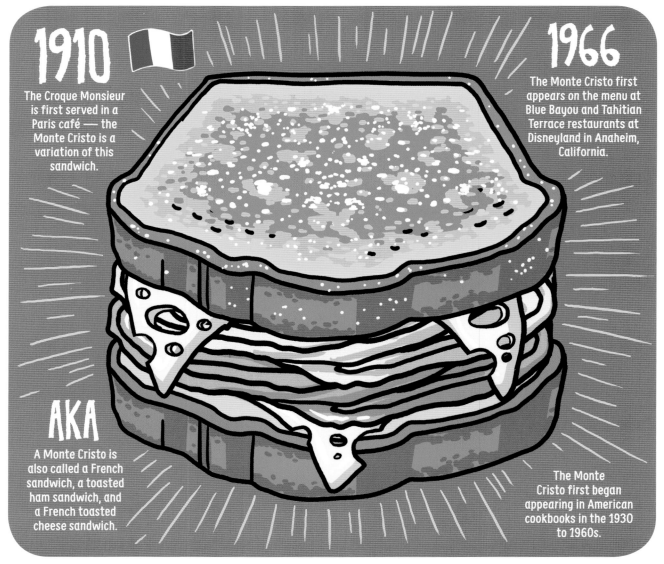

1910

The Croque Monsieur is first served in a Paris café — the Monte Cristo is a variation of this sandwich.

1966

The Monte Cristo first appears on the menu at Blue Bayou and Tahitian Terrace restaurants at Disneyland in Anaheim, California.

AKA

A Monte Cristo is also called a French sandwich, a toasted ham sandwich, and a French toasted cheese sandwich.

The Monte Cristo first began appearing in American cookbooks in the 1930 to 1960s.

FRENCH TOAST

Don't forget to butter the outside of your bread before grilling! (This will only work on flat bread, not a croissant.)

SWISS CHEESE

The Croque Monsieur, French for "Crispy Mister," is rumored to have been accidentally created when two French workers accidentally left their lunch pails, full of ham and cheese sandwiches, too close to a hot radiator.

TURKEY

HAM

FRENCH TOAST RECIPE

The Monte Cristo is easy to make using leftover French toast. The bread has time to cool and firm up before being used as a sandwich base. But if you're running short on leftovers and want to make your own, it's simple!

SWISS CHEESE

4 slices of bread (day old is best)
1 egg
1/2 tsp. cinnamon
1 tsp. vanilla
1/4 cup milk

FRENCH TOAST

Whisk egg, milk, vanilla, and cinnamon together in a shallow bowl. Dip bread into mixture, coating both sides evenly. Cook bread in a hot skillet until both sides are browned. Enjoy!

Grill your sandwich for a couple minutes on each side, until the bread is golden-brown and the toppings are melted.

Don't forget the powdered sugar!

Try your Monte Cristo with a side of sweet jam for dipping!

MONTE CRISTO

REUBEN

The origin of the Reuben sandwich involves a tale of two Reubens — Arnold Reuben, owner of Reuben's Restaurant and Delicatessen in New York City, and Reuben Kulakofsky, a member of a weekly poker group at the Blackstone Hotel in Omaha, Nebraska. Both men have been credited with creating the first Reuben sandwich. Whoever was behind the original, this combination of corned beef, Swiss cheese, sauerkraut, and Russian dressing piled high between two slices of rye bread is a classic.

Despite its name, Russian dressing actually originated in the United States. It was invented by James E. Colburn of Nashua, New Hampshire.

1925

Reuben Kulakofsky is said to have invented the sandwich to feed hungry poker players around midnight during a weekly game at Blackstone Hotel.

MARCH 14

Reuben Sandwich Day in Omaha, Nebraska

1914

The year Reuben's Restaurant in New York, New York, claims to have invented the first Reuben sandwich.

NE

1937

The first appearance of a Reuben sandwich on an official menu — this was at the Cornhusker Hotel in Lincoln, Nebraska.

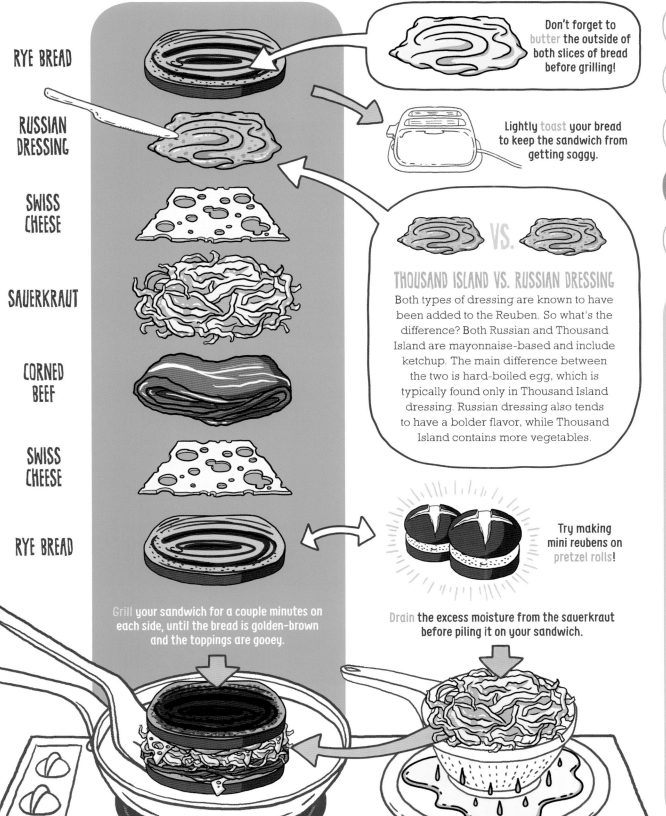

RYE BREAD

RUSSIAN DRESSING

SWISS CHEESE

SAUERKRAUT

CORNED BEEF

SWISS CHEESE

RYE BREAD

Don't forget to butter the outside of both slices of bread before grilling!

Lightly toast your bread to keep the sandwich from getting soggy.

VS.

THOUSAND ISLAND VS. RUSSIAN DRESSING

Both types of dressing are known to have been added to the Reuben. So what's the difference? Both Russian and Thousand Island are mayonnaise-based and include ketchup. The main difference between the two is hard-boiled egg, which is typically found only in Thousand Island dressing. Russian dressing also tends to have a bolder flavor, while Thousand Island contains more vegetables.

Try making mini reubens on pretzel rolls!

Grill your sandwich for a couple minutes on each side, until the bread is golden-brown and the toppings are gooey.

Drain the excess moisture from the sauerkraut before piling it on your sandwich.

REUBEN

VERMONTER

A local favorite out of Burlington, Vermont, the Vermonter is a sandwich that's all about the local ingredients, namely delicious sharp Vermont white cheddar. This sweet-and-savory sammie also features an irresistible combination of ham, turkey, tart green apples, and honey mustard, all grilled together between thick cinnamon raisin bread.

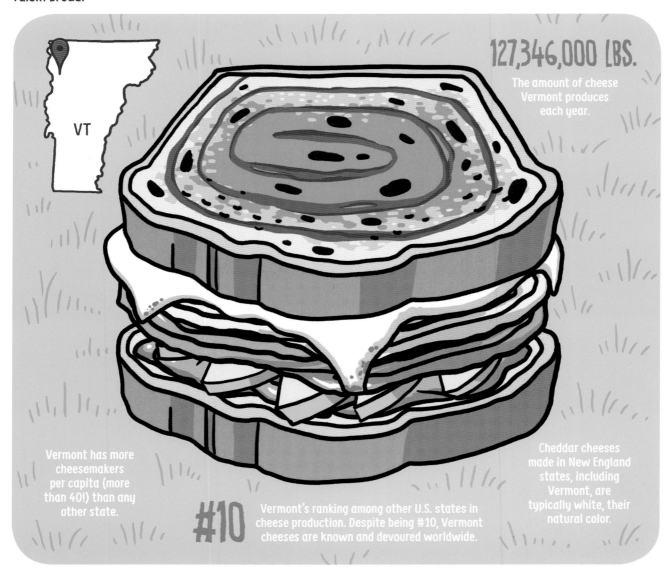

VT

127,346,000 LBS.
The amount of cheese Vermont produces each year.

Vermont has more cheesemakers per capita (more than 40!) than any other state.

#10 Vermont's ranking among other U.S. states in cheese production. Despite being #10, Vermont cheeses are known and devoured worldwide.

Cheddar cheeses made in New England states, including Vermont, are typically white, their natural color.

CINNAMON RAISIN BREAD

WHITE CHEDDAR CHEESE

TURKEY

HAM

GREEN APPLE

HONEY MUSTARD

CINNAMON RAISIN BREAD

Grill your sandwich for a couple minutes on each side, until the bread is golden-brown and the toppings are melty.

Don't forget to butter the outside of both slices of bread before grilling!

OR: Try using apple butter (in place of regular butter) on the outside of your sandwich before grilling for an extra-sweet treat.

1990s

When the Vermonter first originated at Sweetwater's, a popular Burlington restaurant. Cook and waiter Jason Maroney was the man behind the soon-to-be famous sammie.

Serve with another New England classic: salt and vinegar potato chips.

1

2

3

4

5

VERMONTER

CUBAN

Whether you call it a Cuban, a Cubano, a Cuban mix, or even a mixito, this regional sandwich is instantly recognizable. But where it originated in the U.S. is hotly debated. Both Tampa and Miami, Florida, claim this regional treat as their own. Most historians side with team Tampa. When cigar factories popped up in Key West, Florida, and later moved to the Ybor City neighborhood in Tampa. Restaurants near the factories started serving the Cuban to feed workers, and it became so popular it eventually appeared in other Cuban communities in Florida, including Miami.

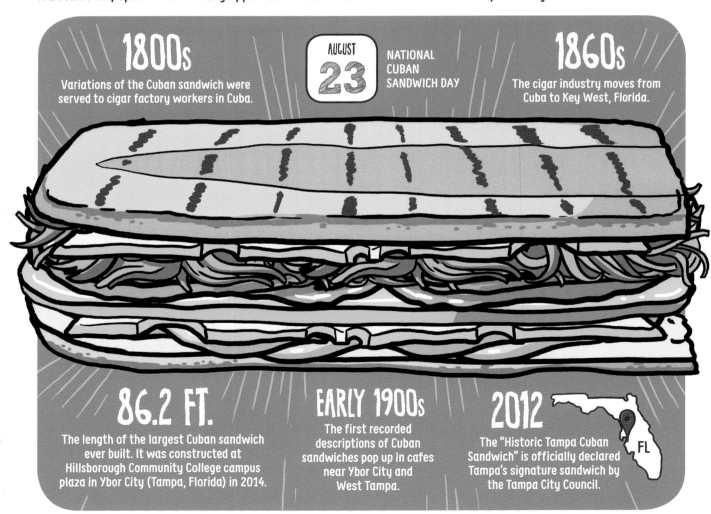

1800s
Variations of the Cuban sandwich were served to cigar factory workers in Cuba.

AUGUST 23
NATIONAL CUBAN SANDWICH DAY

1860s
The cigar industry moves from Cuba to Key West, Florida.

86.2 FT.
The length of the largest Cuban sandwich ever built. It was constructed at Hillsborough Community College campus plaza in Ybor City (Tampa, Florida) in 2014.

EARLY 1900s
The first recorded descriptions of Cuban sandwiches pop up in cafes near Ybor City and West Tampa.

2012
The "Historic Tampa Cuban Sandwich" is officially declared Tampa's signature sandwich by the Tampa City Council.

FL

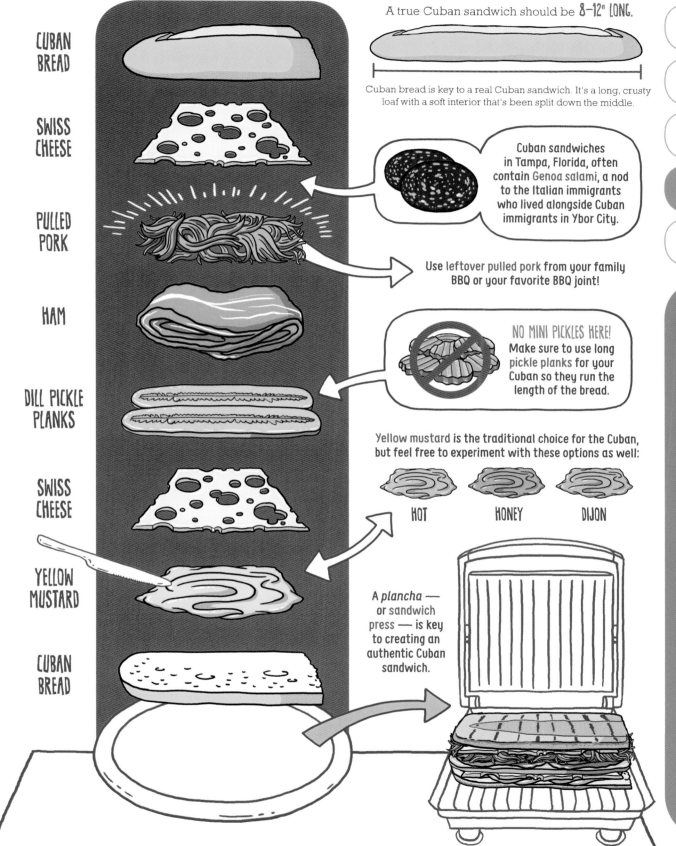

CUBAN BREAD

SWISS CHEESE

PULLED PORK

HAM

DILL PICKLE PLANKS

SWISS CHEESE

YELLOW MUSTARD

CUBAN BREAD

A true Cuban sandwich should be 8–12" LONG.

Cuban bread is key to a real Cuban sandwich. It's a long, crusty loaf with a soft interior that's been split down the middle.

Cuban sandwiches in Tampa, Florida, often contain Genoa salami, a nod to the Italian immigrants who lived alongside Cuban immigrants in Ybor City.

Use leftover pulled pork from your family BBQ or your favorite BBQ joint!

NO MINI PICKLES HERE!
Make sure to use long pickle planks for your Cuban so they run the length of the bread.

Yellow mustard is the traditional choice for the Cuban, but feel free to experiment with these options as well:

HOT   HONEY   DIJON

A *plancha* — or sandwich press — is key to creating an authentic Cuban sandwich.

CUBAN

LEVEL 5

THE BIG TIME
EXTRA COOKING, RECIPES & PREP WORK

You did it! You made it to Level 5 — aka the BIG TIME. This section will be a culmination of your cooking skills. Here you'll find sandwiches that might require some extra prep working or additional cooking. Things like the egg salad sandwich, which — as you might have guessed — requires you to make the egg salad before you can make the sandwich. Or a sloppy joe, which needs to have the meat cooked before the sandwich is assembled.

But never fear! All the tools you'll need to use in this section are pictured to the right, and we've included all the recipes you'll need, along with the sandwich assembly guide, on each page. A sandwich fanatic like you can handle it!

As you eat your way through the final level, keep in mind all the toaster, microwave, oven, and stove safety tips you've learned up until this point. You may want to take another look at sharp knife safety before you start slicing and dicing too. Always ask an adult for help if you don't know how to do something. And most importantly, enjoy eating!

EGG AND CHEESE

Breakfast is the most important meal of the day, but this egg and cheese sandwich isn't strictly an early morning treat — you can make and eat this cheesy delight morning, noon, or night! The best part? You can customize your sandwich however you'd like. While this version is vegetarian, you can add bacon, ham, or sausage if you're a meat eater. Or load up on veggies!

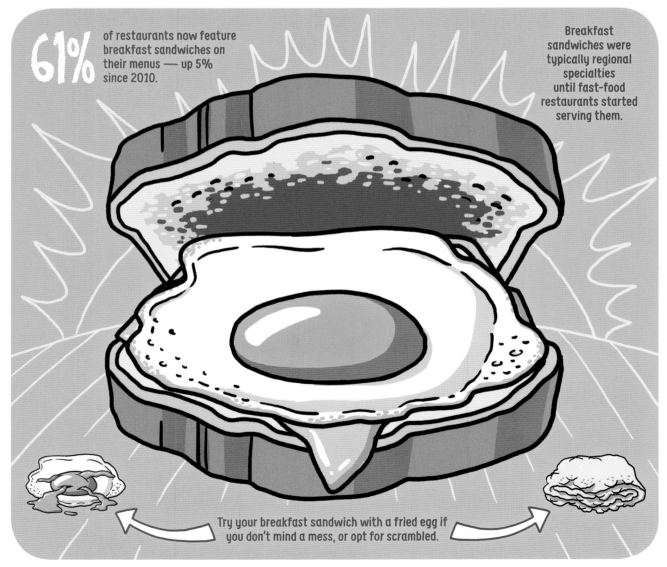

61% of restaurants now feature breakfast sandwiches on their menus — up 5% since 2010.

Breakfast sandwiches were typically regional specialties until fast-food restaurants started serving them.

Try your breakfast sandwich with a fried egg if you don't mind a mess, or opt for scrambled.

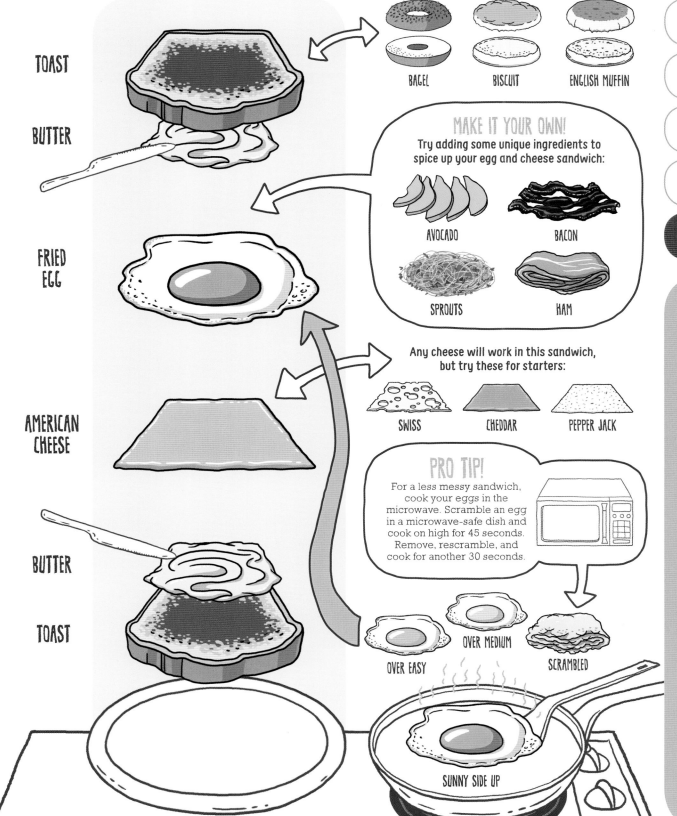

TOAST

BUTTER

FRIED EGG

AMERICAN CHEESE

BUTTER

TOAST

BAGEL

BISCUIT

ENGLISH MUFFIN

MAKE IT YOUR OWN!
Try adding some unique ingredients to spice up your egg and cheese sandwich:

AVOCADO

BACON

SPROUTS

HAM

Any cheese will work in this sandwich, but try these for starters:

SWISS

CHEDDAR

PEPPER JACK

PRO TIP!
For a less messy sandwich, cook your eggs in the microwave. Scramble an egg in a microwave-safe dish and cook on high for 45 seconds. Remove, rescramble, and cook for another 30 seconds.

OVER EASY

OVER MEDIUM

SCRAMBLED

SUNNY SIDE UP

THE HISTORY OF THE EGG SANDWICH

Journey with us down the egg sandwich timeline:

19TH CEN. — London factory workers grab breakfast sandwiches from street vendors on their way to work. These are originally called "bap" sandwiches after the rolls used to hold the fillings.

POST CIVIL WAR — American pioneers eat breakfast sandwiches on their long westward journeys, although the sandwiches aren't reserved as breakfast food. (And the added ingredients are likely a way to disguise less-than-fresh eggs.)

1897 — The first known "breakfast sandwich" recipe, using stale bread, chopped meat, milk, and egg, is published in an American cookbook, *Breakfast, Dinner and Supper, or What to Eat and How to Prepare It.*

1969 — Jack in the Box starts serving up an egg, meat, and cheese breakfast sandwich on an English muffin.

1971 — Herb Peterson, an advertising executive, invents the Egg McMuffin and starts selling it at his restaurant. He later introduces the sandwich to McDonald's chairman Ray Kroc.

1972 — The Egg McMuffin hits the McDonald's menu, making the breakfast sandwich a nationwide favorite.

WE DARE YOU!

An egg sandwich is great on its own, but a sandwich savant like you is probably ready to take it to the next level. Think you can handle the weird, the gross, the amazing, and everything in between? Here are just a few out-there options to experiment with . . . if you dare!

MAPLE SYRUP

SRIRACHA

MARSHMALLOWS

JALAPEÑO MUSTARD

PICKLE RELISH

RADISH

SPAGHETTI

BRUSSELS SPROUTS

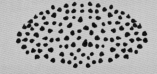

CHOCOLATE CHIPS

BANANAS

TUNA SALAD

Tuna salad is just about as easy as cooking gets. All you really need is canned tuna and mayonnaise and you've got yourself a meal. Use less mayo if you prefer a drier tuna salad, or use more for a smoother, creamier texture. Add some salt and pepper, and voilà! If you're feeling fancy, try adding pickle relish or hardboiled eggs.

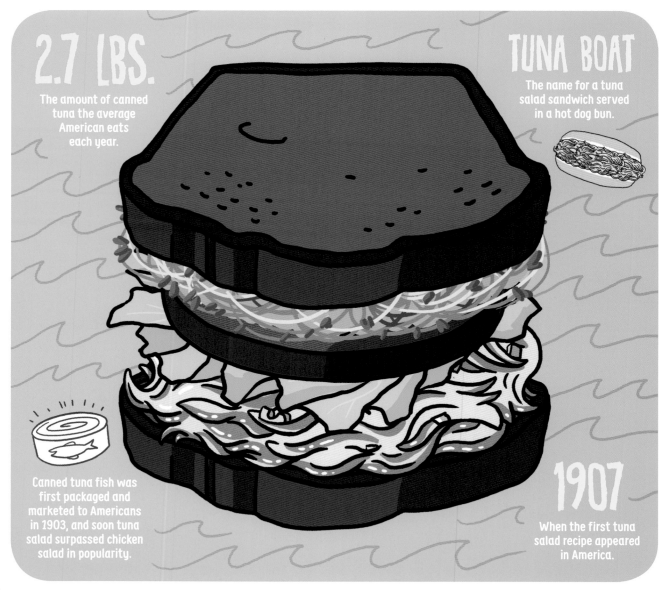

2.7 LBS.
The amount of canned tuna the average American eats each year.

TUNA BOAT
The name for a tuna salad sandwich served in a hot dog bun.

Canned tuna fish was first packaged and marketed to Americans in 1903, and soon tuna salad surpassed chicken salad in popularity.

1907
When the first tuna salad recipe appeared in America.

WHEAT BREAD

Add avocado to make your sandwich extra creamy.

You can even serve your tuna salad in half an avocado — not a sandwich, but still delicious!

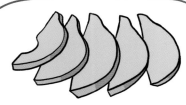

SPROUTS

TOMATO

LETTUCE

Want some extra crunch? Try adding sliced cucumbers to your sandwich.

TUNA SALAD

Use yogurt instead of mayo for a lighter tuna salad.

WHEAT BREAD

Mix with:
2–4 Tbs. mayo
1 Tbs. lemon juice
Salt and pepper to taste

EASY TUNA SALAD

2 cans of tuna fish	1 piece of celery	1/4 of a small onion

Finely dice celery and onion.

Mix all ingredients together, using as much mayo and salt and pepper as you prefer.

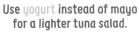

TUNA SALAD

TUNA MELT

Tuna salad not enough for you? Take your tuna sandwich to the next level by turning up the heat — literally. Whip up your basic tuna salad, then pile it onto your base of choice and top the whole thing with cheese. Pop it into the oven or toaster oven to make things melty, and then enjoy!

2013
Up until this year, tuna held the title of America's favorite fish.

1989
The height of canned tuna consumption in the U.S. Americans ate nearly 4 lbs. per person that year.

Before 1900, canned tuna was practically nonexistent in the United States.

TOASTIE
Another name used in Australia, New Zealand, and the U.K. for a melt sandwich — this would be a tuna toastie!

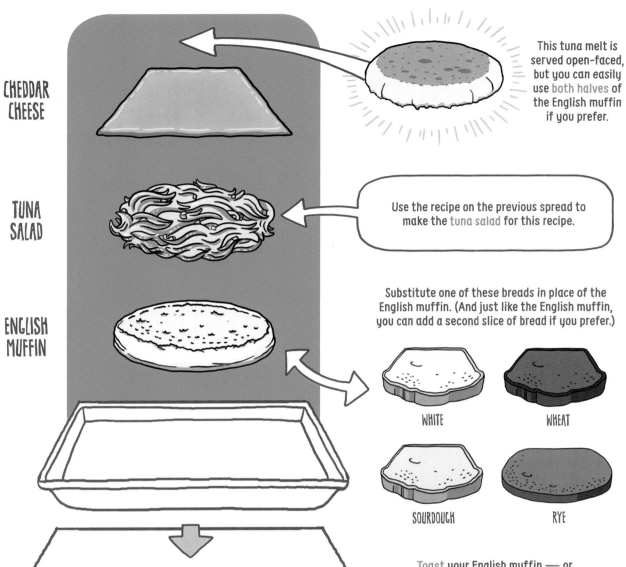

CHEDDAR CHEESE

This tuna melt is served open-faced, but you can easily use both halves of the English muffin if you prefer.

TUNA SALAD

Use the recipe on the previous spread to make the tuna salad for this recipe.

ENGLISH MUFFIN

Substitute one of these breads in place of the English muffin. (And just like the English muffin, you can add a second slice of bread if you prefer.)

WHITE

WHEAT

SOURDOUGH

RYE

Once you've assembled your tuna melt, a few minutes under the broiler will do the trick!

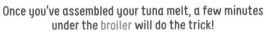

TIMER
2:50

BROIL   HI

Toast your English muffin — or bread if you prefer — before piling on the tuna salad and cheese.

TUNA MELT

CHICKEN SALAD

Can a salad and a sandwich ever coexist? In this case they can! Chicken salad is easy to make using leftover chicken. Don't have any in the fridge? A rotisserie chicken from the grocery store works just as well. And the beauty of this salad-sandwich hybrid is it can be eaten cold. Just whip up your chicken salad in advance, pile it onto your bread of choice, and eat! Easy to assemble and even easier to enjoy.

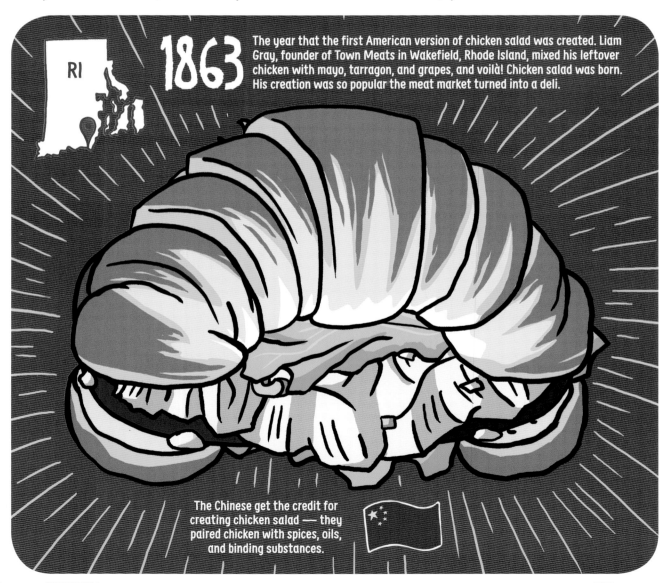

RI

1863
The year that the first American version of chicken salad was created. Liam Gray, founder of Town Meats in Wakefield, Rhode Island, mixed his leftover chicken with mayo, tarragon, and grapes, and voilà! Chicken salad was born. His creation was so popular the meat market turned into a deli.

The Chinese get the credit for creating chicken salad — they paired chicken with spices, oils, and binding substances.

CROISSANT

TOMATO

LETTUCE

CHICKEN SALAD

CROISSANT

A croissant fancies up this sandwich, but you can just as easily use two slices of bread — or one if you prefer your sandwich open-faced.

CUSTOMIZE IT!

Chicken salad is easy to customize — add curry powder for an interesting twist on the classic, or dried cherries for a sweeter version. You can also add grapes, apples, or almonds.

Use yogurt instead of mayo for a lighter chicken salad.

Mix with:
1/2 cup mayo
Salt and pepper to taste

Refrigerate for a few hours (or overnight) to let the flavors settle.

EASY CHICKEN SALAD

1 1/2 cups chopped cooked chicken

1 stalk of celery, chopped

1 small onion, finely chopped

Chop chicken, celery, and onion.

You can also add other herbs or spices to "spice" up the mixture.

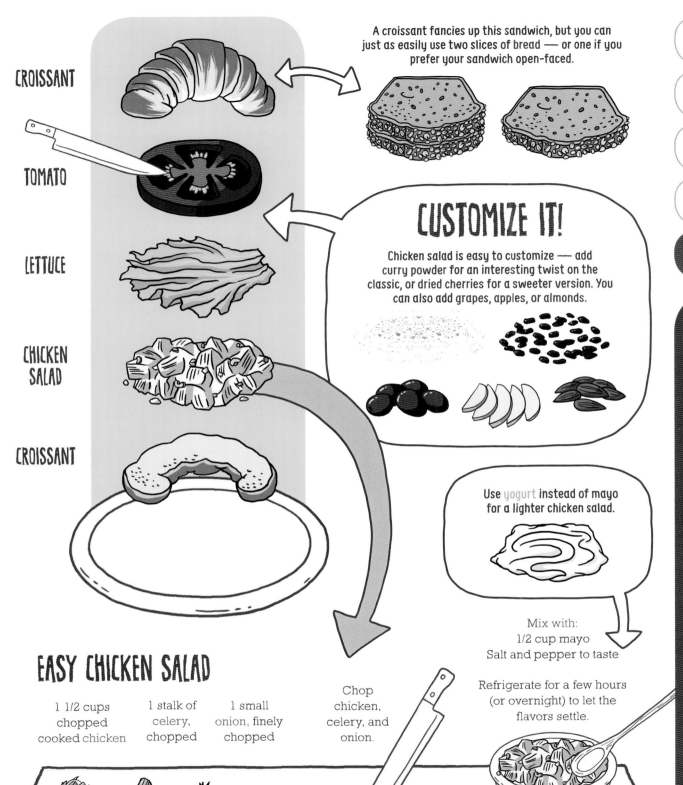

EGG SALAD

Egg salad is easy to make, and there's good news for sandwich-lovers everywhere — an egg salad sandwich is just as easy! Take basic egg salad, slap it between two slices of bread, and you're good to go. You can also dress it up however you'd like — adding lettuce and tomato to your sandwich, or spicing up the egg salad itself. Try adding curry powder to your egg salad recipe for a unique take on the traditional recipe.

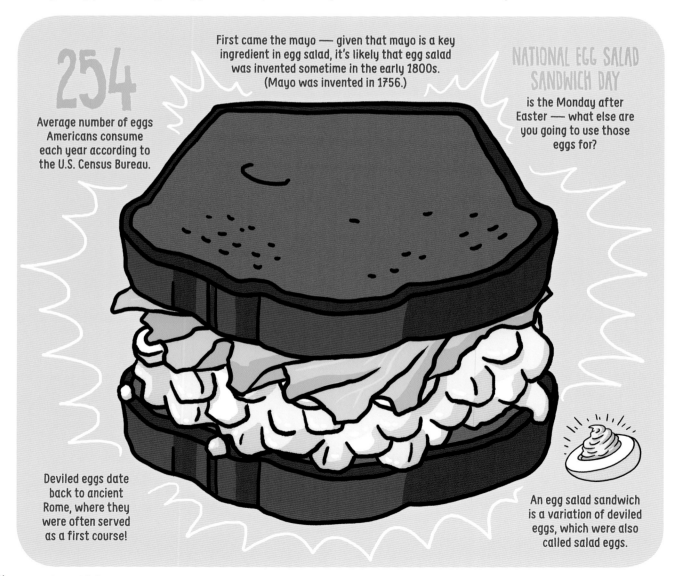

254
Average number of eggs Americans consume each year according to the U.S. Census Bureau.

First came the mayo — given that mayo is a key ingredient in egg salad, it's likely that egg salad was invented sometime in the early 1800s. (Mayo was invented in 1756.)

NATIONAL EGG SALAD SANDWICH DAY
is the Monday after Easter — what else are you going to use those eggs for?

Deviled eggs date back to ancient Rome, where they were often served as a first course!

An egg salad sandwich is a variation of deviled eggs, which were also called salad eggs.

WHEAT BREAD

Swap out the bread entirely and opt for a pita pocket — easier to eat on the go.

Or try it in a lettuce wrap!

Spice it up with **HOT SAUCE!**

LETTUCE

You can also spice up your sandwich by adding:

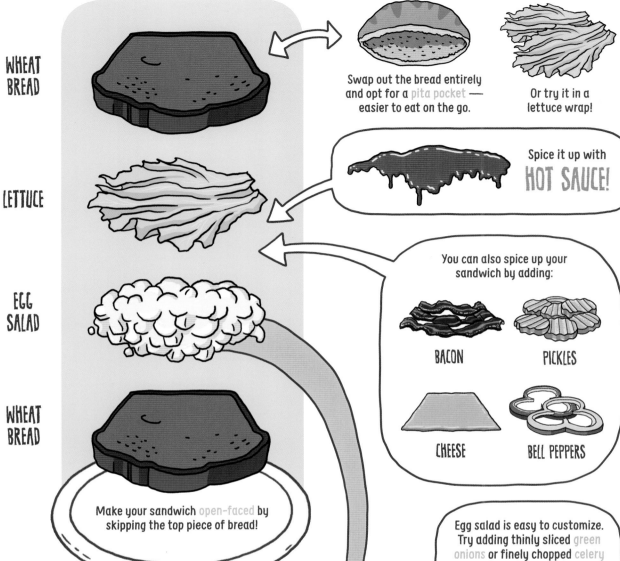

BACON

PICKLES

EGG SALAD

CHEESE

BELL PEPPERS

WHEAT BREAD

Make your sandwich open-faced by skipping the top piece of bread!

Egg salad is easy to customize. Try adding thinly sliced green onions or finely chopped celery for extra crunch and color. And if you don't like mayo, Greek yogurt is an easy substitute!

BASIC EGG SALAD

In a medium saucepan, cover 6 eggs with at least an inch of water. Bring to a boil and remove from heat. Let the eggs sit in the hot water for 15 minutes, then run them under cool water.

Peel and chop the eggs.

Mix with:
1/4 cup mayo
1 tablespoon mustard
Salt and pepper to taste

Refrigerate for at least an hour.

EGG SALAD

APPLE PIE

There's nothing like a warm slice of homemade apple pie. Now imagine you could hold that pie in your hand and enjoy it for lunch. Thanks to this apple pie sandwich, you can! To make things easy, you can use store-bought apple pie filling, or if you're feeling fancy try making your own. (Just remember to ask an adult to help you when you're using knives or the stove.)

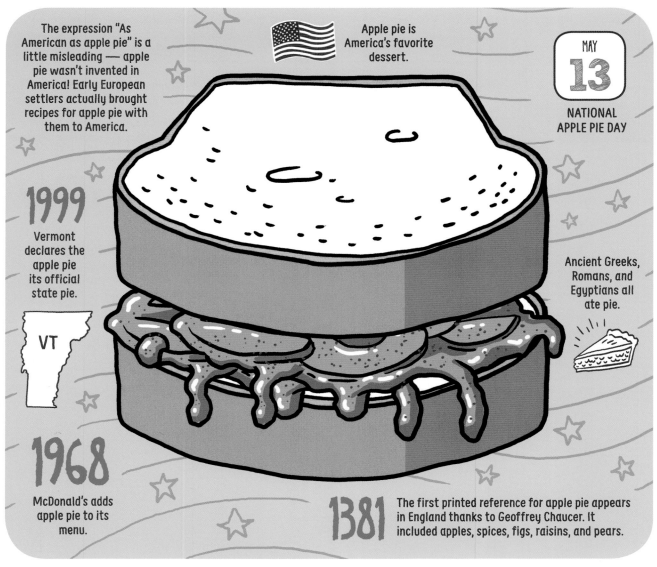

The expression "As American as apple pie" is a little misleading — apple pie wasn't invented in America! Early European settlers actually brought recipes for apple pie with them to America.

Apple pie is America's favorite dessert.

MAY
13

NATIONAL APPLE PIE DAY

1999

Vermont declares the apple pie its official state pie.

VT

Ancient Greeks, Romans, and Egyptians all ate pie.

1968

McDonald's adds apple pie to its menu.

1381

The first printed reference for apple pie appears in England thanks to Geoffrey Chaucer. It included apples, spices, figs, raisins, and pears.

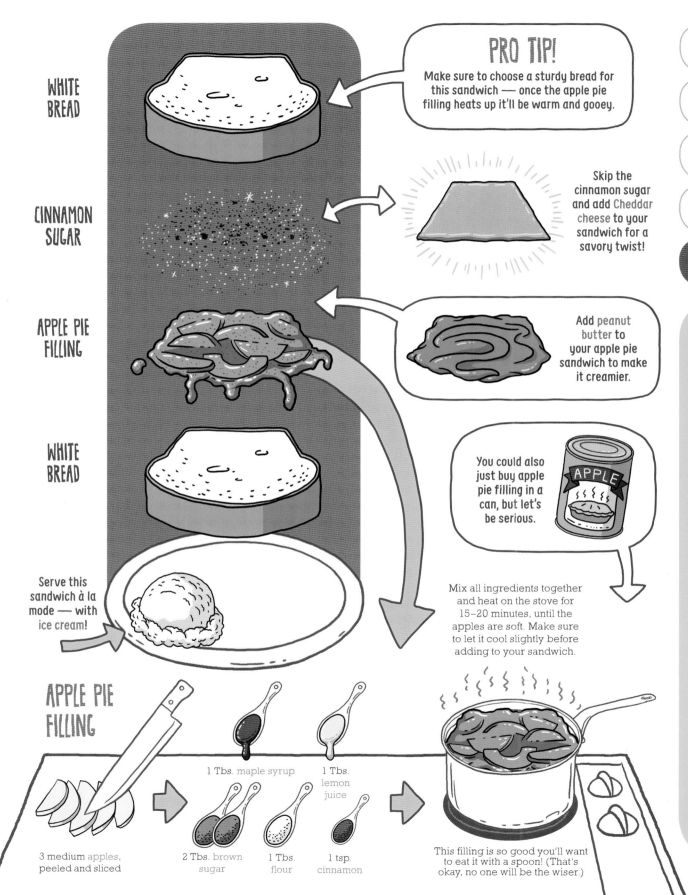

WHITE BREAD

PRO TIP!
Make sure to choose a sturdy bread for this sandwich — once the apple pie filling heats up it'll be warm and gooey.

CINNAMON SUGAR

Skip the cinnamon sugar and add Cheddar cheese to your sandwich for a savory twist!

APPLE PIE FILLING

Add peanut butter to your apple pie sandwich to make it creamier.

WHITE BREAD

You could also just buy apple pie filling in a can, but let's be serious.

APPLE

Serve this sandwich à la mode — with ice cream!

Mix all ingredients together and heat on the stove for 15–20 minutes, until the apples are soft. Make sure to let it cool slightly before adding to your sandwich.

APPLE PIE FILLING

1 Tbs. maple syrup

1 Tbs. lemon juice

3 medium apples, peeled and sliced

2 Tbs. brown sugar

1 Tbs. flour

1 tsp. cinnamon

This filling is so good you'll want to eat it with a spoon! (That's okay, no one will be the wiser.)

SLOPPY JOE

Sloppy, savory, delicious — all the hallmarks of a truly awesome sandwich. And no sandwich embodies those attributes better than a good ol' sloppy joe. This sandwich is versatile too and easy to adapt if you don't eat red meat. Just substitute ground turkey or chicken in place of ground beef.

1933

The year Sloppy Joe's Bar opened in Key West, Florida — they've been serving sloppy joes ever since.

CUBA

HAVANA, CUBA
Home of the original Sloppy Joe's Bar

Originally, mixing ground meat with sauces was a way to make it last longer — especially helpful during WWII.

MARCH 18
National Sloppy Joe Day.

1969
The year Hunt's introduced Manwich — aka sloppy joe sauce in a can.

HAMBURGER BUN

PICKLES

GROUND MEAT MIXTURE

WHAT'S IN A NAME?
Legend has it sloppy joes got their name way back in 1930 thanks to a cook named Joe at Floyd Angell's cafe in Sioux City, Iowa. Joe added tomato sauce to his "loose meat" sandwiches — popular in the Midwest at the time — and the "sloppy joe" was born!

Try the Sloppy Joe Grilled Cheese — **a step up from an uncomplicated classic. Just substitute white or wheat bread for the bun, add some cheese, and grill it up!**

Serve on smaller buns **or** Hawaiian rolls **to make sloppy joe sliders!**

You can also add veggies to the mix — try carrots, onions, diced tomatoes, celery, bell peppers, mushrooms, or garlic.

HOMEMADE SLOPPY JOES

Brown your ground meat in a pan on the stove, stirring until fully cooked. Add all the other ingredients and pile onto a bun.

3/4 cup ketchup

1/4 cup mustard

2 Tbs. Worcestershire sauce

1 pound ground beef

2 Tbs. brown sugar

*If you want to go the easy route, just add one can of sloppy joe sauce, like Manwich, to your cooked ground meat.

SLOPPY JOE

FRENCH DIP

A distant cousin of the Italian beef, the French dip is yet another sandwich with hotly debated origins. In fact, despite having "French" in its name, the French dip isn't French at all! The name only refers to the French baguette on which it's served. This uniquely American creation, first created in California, features loads of tender roast beef in the middle, is also served with a side of au jus in which to dip the sandwich.

LOS ANGELES
Birthplace of the French dip.

CA

1908
The year Cole's Pacific Electric Buffet and Phillipe the Original, two Los Angeles restaurants, opened. Both claim to have invented the French dip.

AU JUS
French for "with juice"

1918
The year Phillipe's claims its owner, Philippe Mathieu, invented the French dip.

FRENCH BAGUETTE

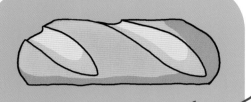

 Add mayo for extra creaminess.

 Or try horseradish for extra zip!

SAUTÉED ONIONS

PRO TIP!

Leftover roast beef finds new life in the French dip — just make sure to slice the meat thinly before piling it on the bread. Don't have leftovers? You can buy cooked roast beef at the grocery store or deli to make it easy.

ROAST BEEF

EASY AU JUS RECIPE

You can buy au jus gravy mix at the store, or try your hand at making your own!

3 cups beef broth
1 tsp. soy sauce
salt and pepper

Heat beef broth and stir in remaining ingredients, adding salt and pepper to taste. If you like your au jus slightly thicker, whisk a few tbs. of flour to the mixture.

FRENCH BAGUETTE

Serve with a side of au jus for dipping, along with a side of french fries.
(French dip, french fries, why not?)

WESTERN

A Western sandwich, also known as a Denver sandwich, is custom made to be eaten for breakfast. That's because the Western sandwich is literally a Western omelet — scrambled eggs, ham, cheese, onion, and green pepper — sandwiched between two slices of bread. But believe it or not, the Western sandwich actually came *before* the Western omelet!

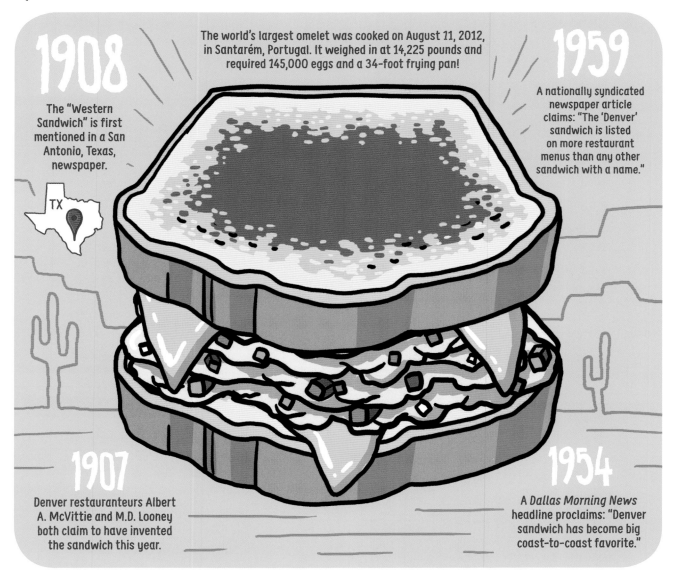

1908
The "Western Sandwich" is first mentioned in a San Antonio, Texas, newspaper.

TX

The world's largest omelet was cooked on August 11, 2012, in Santarém, Portugal. It weighed in at 14,225 pounds and required 145,000 eggs and a 34-foot frying pan!

1959
A nationally syndicated newspaper article claims: "The 'Denver' sandwich is listed on more restaurant menus than any other sandwich with a name."

1907
Denver restauranteurs Albert A. McVittie and M.D. Looney both claim to have invented the sandwich this year.

1954
A *Dallas Morning News* headline proclaims: "Denver sandwich has become big coast-to-coast favorite."

SOURDOUGH TOAST

Make sure to use toasted bread for your sandwich — untoasted won't hold up to your omelet.

AMERICAN CHEESE

DID YOU KNOW?

The Denver omelet might have its roots in the Mile-High City, but the word *omelette* itself is actually French in origin. The spelling we're used to seeing started appearing as far back as the 17th century, but other versions, including **alumelle** and **alumete**, were used as early as 1393.

DENVER OMELET

American cheese is the old standby here, but any cheese will work in this sandwich. Try these for starters:

CHEDDAR   PEPPER JACK

COLBY JACK   PROVOLONE

AMERICAN CHEESE

SOURDOUGH TOAST

FACT:
Oddly enough, finding a Denver sandwich in Denver is virtually impossible!

Serve with hash browns for a real breakfast experience!

WESTERN OMELET

Mix with 2 eggs and a splash of milk.

Salt and pepper to taste.

Pour egg mixture into frying pan and cook on medium heat until set — don't overcook!

2 slices of ham | 1 green pepper | 1 small onion | Chop ham, pepper, onion.

CHEESESTEAK

Philadelphia is famous for a number of things, but among sandwich aficionados one thing stands out — the cheesesteak. Often known as a Philadelphia cheesesteak or Philly cheesesteak, this is a sandwich worth making a pilgrimage for. Not ready to head to the East Coast? Never fear! You can whip up this meaty, cheesy delight in your own kitchen. And you should. Because let's face it, almost everything tastes better with cheese, and the same holds true for sandwiches.

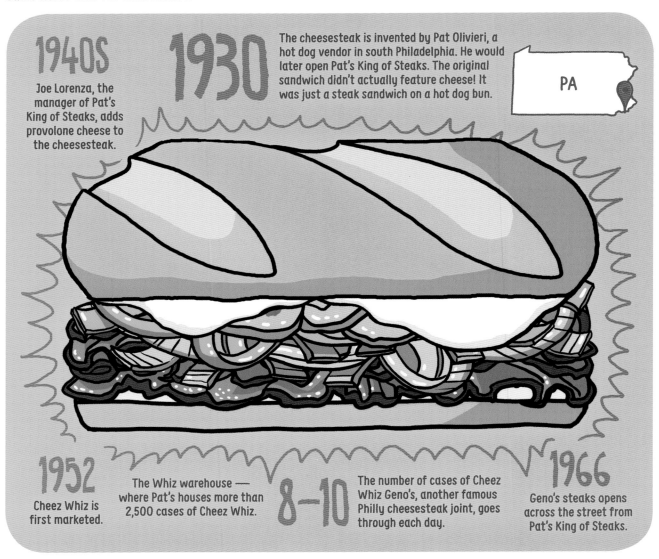

1940S

Joe Lorenza, the manager of Pat's King of Steaks, adds provolone cheese to the cheesesteak.

1930

The cheesesteak is invented by Pat Olivieri, a hot dog vendor in south Philadelphia. He would later open Pat's King of Steaks. The original sandwich didn't actually feature cheese! It was just a steak sandwich on a hot dog bun.

PA

1952

Cheez Whiz is first marketed.

The Whiz warehouse — where Pat's houses more than 2,500 cases of Cheez Whiz.

8–10

The number of cases of Cheez Whiz Geno's, another famous Philly cheesesteak joint, goes through each day.

1966

Geno's steaks opens across the street from Pat's King of Steaks.

FRENCH BAGUETTE

You don't have to stick with French bread — any long, crusty roll will do. Feeling brave? Switch it up with a round roll, a panini, a wrap, or even an English muffin!

PROVOLONE CHEESE

SAUTÉED MUSHROOMS

THE GREAT CHEESE DEBATE

The cheesesteak typically comes with one of two types of cheese — provolone or Cheez Whiz. But which is correct is hotly debated. Cheez Whiz offered a quick, easy alternative when it was first introduced, but that wasn't until the 1950s. In fact, the original cheese debate was between American and provolone. Nowadays, Whiz is the favorite for customers at both Pat's and Geno's, the most famous of the Philly cheesesteak joints. But if you ask us, provolone — aka real cheese! — is best. But don't take our word for it. Experiment with your sandwich and try both versions!

GRILLED PEPPERS

GRILLED ONIONS

STEAK

FRENCH BAGUETTE

Try a chicken cheesesteak — just substitute grilled chicken for the steak.

Skirt steak, onion, green peppers, and mushrooms

Chop together to make it easy.

Sauté in pan until meat is cooked through, about 5 minutes.

PO' BOY

A southern staple, the po' boy comes to us from deep in the heart of Louisiana — New Orleans, to be specific. A traditional po' boy is made with fried seafood — shrimp, oysters, crab, and crawfish are all possibilities — and can be served hot or cold. A po' boy can also be made with roast beef. But no matter the filling, a po' boy is always served on a French baguette, crispy on the outside and soft in the center.

LA

1929 The po' boy was created in New Orleans, Louisiana.

In New Orleans, "Vietnamese po' boy" is another name for a banh mi sandwich.

A "dressed" po' boy has romaine lettuce, tomato, pickles, and mayo.

The trademark of a po' boy is fresh, delicious French bread.

OYSTER LOAVES The name for fried oyster sandwiches on French bread, similar to po' boys, served in the late 1800s in New Orleans and San Francisco.

TOASTED
BAGUETTE

RÉMOULADE
SAUCE

CAJUN
SEASONING

FRIED
SHRIMP

LETTUCE

TOASTED
BAGUETTE

ALL ABOUT THE PO' BOY

The name po' boy is a shortened version of "poor boy" and refers to the fact that the sandwich was originally a very inexpensive way to get a solid, filling meal. So who coined the term, and why? That would be Benny and Clovis Martin, brothers, restaurant owners, and former streetcar conductors in New Orleans. In 1929, approximately 1,800 transit workers went on strike for four months against the streetcar company. The Martin brothers served their former colleagues, who were protesting in the streets, sandwiches free of charge. Restaurant workers jokingly referred to the striking workers as "poor boys" and soon the name was stuck to the sandwiches as well.

Leftover fried shrimp works just fine, or you can use frozen popcorn shrimp.

Try these other fillings too!

OYSTERS

CRAWFISH

CRAB

Brush the cut sides of your baguette with melted butter before toasting.

RÉMOULADE SAUCE

You can buy rémoulade sauce to drizzle on your po' boy, but if you want to go all in, it's easy to make your own!

1/2 cup mayo

1 Tbs. horseradish

1 tsp. pickle relish

1 tsp. minced garlic

1 tsp. cayenne pepper

Mix all ingredients together in a bowl. Drizzle over your sandwich and refrigerate the rest.

ITALIAN BEEF

No trip to the Windy City is complete without an Italian beef sandwich. This Chicago staple takes its name from tender, juicy roast beef, shredded or thinly sliced, that's stuffed inside the sammie. The beef is marinated in its own juices and then piled high on a crusty Italian roll. If you have plenty of napkins — or maybe a shower — handy, you can also get the sandwich "wet" — aka soaked in the drippings, bread and all.

1900S
The Italian beef is created by Italian immigrants working in Chicago's old Union Stock Yards.

1938
The first Al's Beef opens in Chicago, founded by Al Ferreri, his sister Frances, and her husband, Chris Pacelli Sr. They also claim to have invented the Italian beef.

Cooking beef in its own juices was devised as a way to make tougher cuts of meat easier to eat.

A "combo" adds Italian sausage to the sandwich.

1925
The Scala Packing company is founded. The company maintains that its founder, Pasquale Scala, invented the Italian beef sandwich.

The Italian beef was likely created as a way to stretch a small amount of food to feed a large number of people at Italian weddings.

ITALIAN ROLL

BEEF DRIPPINGS

ROASTED PEPPERS

SHREDDED ITALIAN BEEF

ITALIAN ROLL

SWEET VS. HOT

A "sweet" version (used in this recipe) includes roasted sweet red and green peppers (which you can buy in a jar).

A "hot" beef includes hot giardiniera, an Italian relish with peppers and other vegetables.

Add cheese — provolone or mozzarella are best — and turn your Italian beef into a "cheesy beef" or "cheef."

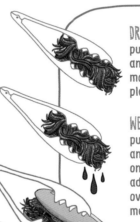

DRY — the beef is pulled from its juices and allowed to drip mostly dry before being placed on the roll.

WET — the beef is pulled from its juices and immediately put onto a roll; you an also add a spoonful of juice over the top of the meat.

DIPPED — the entire sandwich (including the bread) is dipped in beef juice.

EASY ITALIAN BEEF

3 lbs. rump roast

1 package Italian salad dressing

1 can (15-oz.) beef broth

8 oz. pepperoncini (plus juice)

Mix all ingredients together in a crockpot, including about half the juice from the pepperoncini. (Use fewer peppers and less juice if you don't like spice.) Turn crockpot on high, and cook for 4–5 hours, until meat is cooked and tender.

Shred your meat and save the liquid. That's your dipping sauce!

BANH MI

This Vietnamese favorite features loads of fresh herbs and pickled veggies all crammed into a warm, toasty French baguette. And you can't argue that the sandwich isn't accurately named — *banh mi* is a Vietnamese term for all types of bread. This version uses grilled chicken, but a banh mi sandwich can also be made with beef or pork if you prefer. You can even use tofu if you're meat-free. Whatever your protein preference may be, this cultural sandwich is a guaranteed flavor explosion in your mouth.

3/24/2011 The date "banh mi" was added to the *Oxford English Dictionary*.

A banh mi has also been called a Vietnamese po' boy.

Cilantro is a must-have on a banh mi sandwich, but a good chunk of Americans think it tastes like soap.

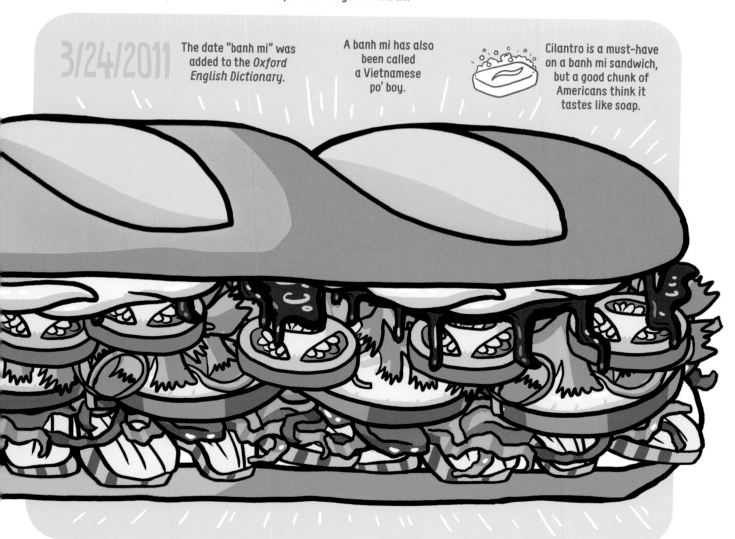

BAGUETTE

MAYO

DRESSING

JALAPEÑOS

CILANTRO

CUCUMBERS

SHREDDED
PICKLED
VEGGIES

GRILLED
CHICKEN

BAGUETTE

DRESSING RECIPE

1 Tbs. fish sauce
1/2 tsp. soy sauce
2 Tbs. vegetable oil

Mix all ingredients and drizzle
on top of your sandwich before
closing it up.

*Don't have fish sauce?
Try substituting Worcestershire
sauce, or soy sauce with a
splash of lime juice.

ARE YOU PART OF
THE 4–14% OF PEOPLE THAT
THINK CILANTRO TASTES LIKE
SOAP? FEEL FREE TO LEAVE IT
OFF YOUR BANH MI IF
THAT'S THE CASE.

Scoop out the inside of your
baguette to create a better
balance between bread and
fillings. Plus, scooping out
your bread creates more room
for fresh, delicious fillings!

Mix together:
1/2 cup rice vinegar
1/2 tsp. salt
1 Tbs. sugar

Toss your shredded veggies with
the vinegar mixture and let sit for 15
minutes. Drain before using.

QUICK PICKLED VEGGIES

Pickled veggies are a hallmark of
banh mi sandwiches, and lucky for
you, they're easy to make! Carrots
and radishes work well here.

Shred your
veggies using
a grater.

ALISON DEERING

Originally from Michigan — the Mitten State! — Alison learned the value of a good book and a great sandwich early on. After earning a journalism degree from the University of Missouri-Columbia, she started her career as a writer and editor. Alison currently lives in Chicago, Illinois, with her husband, where she makes, eats, and talks about as many sandwiches as humanly possible.

If Alison were a sandwich, she would be a fancy grilled cheese, inspired by the Grilled 3 Cheese at Café Muse in Royal Oak, Michigan.

WHOLE GRAIN
BREAD

HAVARTI CHEESE

TOMATO

BASIL

HONEY

FONTINA CHEESE

MOZZARELLA CHEESE

WHOLE GRAIN
BREAD

BOB LENTZ

Bob is an art director who has designed and illustrated many successful books for children, and is the latter half of the duo Lemke & Lentz, creators of *Book-O-Beards*, part of the Wearable Books series. In his spare time, he likes to talk about food, especially sandwiches. Bob lives in Minnesota, with his wife and children, where they go for long walks, sing old-timey songs, and eat ice cream with too many toppings.

If Bob were a sandwich, he would be "The Snowpig," proudly hailing from Morty's at Hyland Hills Ski Area in Bloomington, Minnesota.

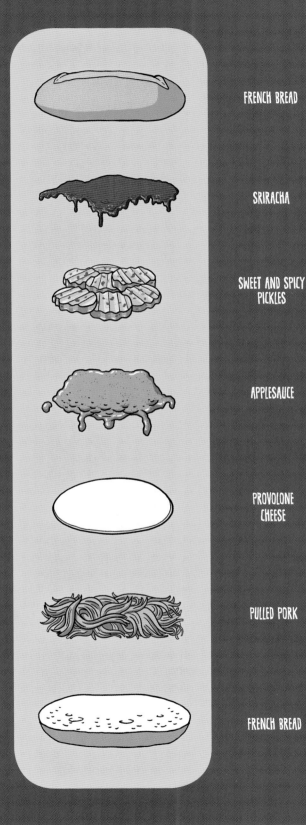

FRENCH BREAD

SRIRACHA

SWEET AND SPICY PICKLES

APPLESAUCE

PROVOLONE CHEESE

PULLED PORK

FRENCH BREAD

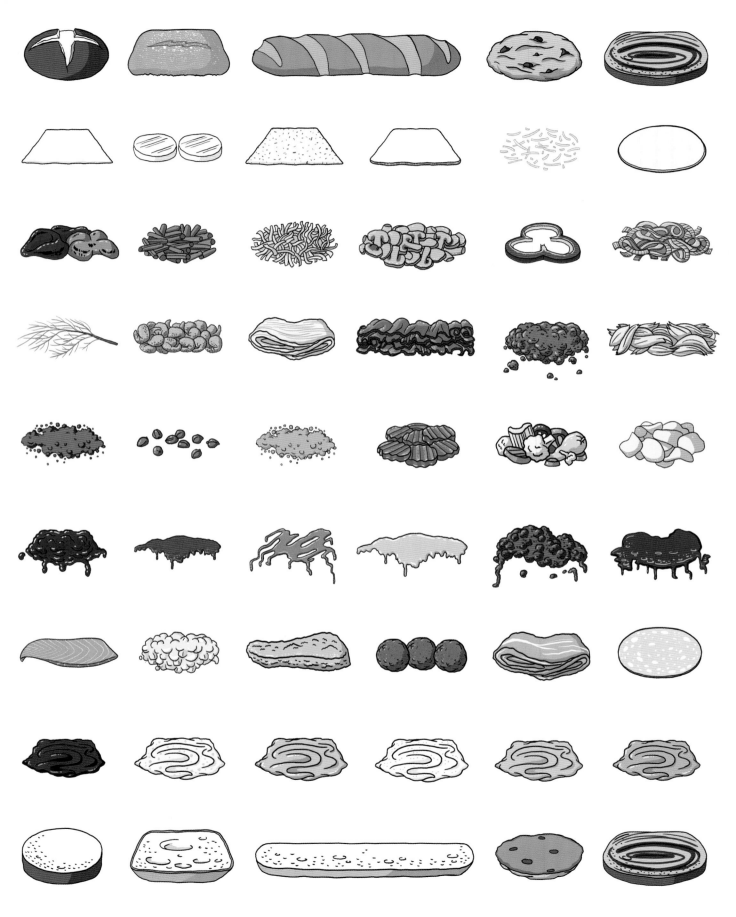